CLAUDIO PESCIO

TUSCANY

EXPLORED THROUGHOUT IN 56 ITINERARIES

440 Colour Illustrations
5   Street Maps
2   Fold-out Views

D1335807

BONECHI EDIZIONI "IL TURISMO"

Reprint 2008

© Copyright by Bonechi Edizioni "Il Turismo" S.r.l
Via G. Di Vittorio, 31 - 50145 Florence (Italy)
Tel. +39-055.37.57.39
Fax +39-055.37.47.01
e-mail: info@bonechionline.com
        bbonechi@dada.it
Internet: http://www.bonechionline.com
Printed in Italy

Photos: Bonechi Edizioni "Il Turismo" S.r.l. Archives; Nestore
Buonafede; Giuliano Corti; Guido Cozzi; Rolando Fusi; Maurizio
Magnelli; pages 93-100 Ditta I-Buga, Milan (Aut. SMA no. 467/74);
page 54: Museo delle Porcellane di Doccia, Sesto Fiorentino; page 61:
Museo Vinciano, Vinci; page 143: Consorzio del Gallo Nero, Florence.
The photo on page 24 (below) was kindly granted by Cassa di Risparmio
di Firenze.
Maps: Studio Biagi & Capaccioli, Florence
Translation: Rosalynd C. Pio and Merry Orling
Photolithography: Fotolito RAF, Florence
Print: Lito Terrazzi, Florence
ISBN 978-88-7204-230-4

View of the magnificent Tuscan countryside.

GENERAL ASPECTS OF TUSCANY

The Tuscan region is mostly hilly and mountainous. The major range running northsouth on the east, the Tusco-Emiliano Apennines, vaunts peaks of respectable heights (e.g., Mt. Prato at 2053 m, Mt. Corno alle Scale at 1945 m, and Mt. Falterona at 1654 m); the Apuane on the west are almost as high. As you go south, the mountains gradually turn into hills (named after the Chianti, Metallifere, and Amiata regions) collectively known as the Antiappennini (pre-Apennines). Valleys of considerable size (Lunigiana, Garfagnana, Mugello, and Casentino) are sandwiched between the Apennines. The rare plains are either of the coastal type (e.g., Versilia and Maremma) or alluvional (e.g., the Arno Valley). The coastline alternates long stretches of beach (Versilia, Cecina) with promontories and cliffs (Piombino, Argentario). The islands of the Tuscan archipelago may be considered a continuation of the geological configuration of the coast. The major Tuscan rivers are the Arno, Ombrone, Serchio, and Sieve, while no lakes worthy of mention exist. In terms of vegetation, there are great chestnut forests in the mountain regions, Mediterranean pines and brush along the coast, with neat olive groves and vineyards covering the hillsides. Subterranean Tuscany also yields rich fruits: mercury (Amiata), copper and alabaster (Colline Metallifere), marble (Apuane, especially Carrara), and iron (Elba and Grosseto). The Larderello geysers near Volterra generate some of the region's electricity. Typical features of Tuscany's winter climate are heavy rainfall and frequent temperature plunges, mainly due to icy north-winds. Summer hot spells are periodically mitigated by sudden rain storms.

Florence - Siege and defeat of Pisa, frescoed by Giorgio Vasari, in the Hall of the Five Hundred in Palazzo Vecchio.

HISTORY

Tuscany, unlike the majority of Italian regions, may be defined as a historic entity unto itself. This is because constant bickering and rivalry did not prevent the Tuscan towns from sharing a common history and language, a heritage they have preserved for two millennia. Tuscan history begins around (1000 B.C.) when the land lying between the Arno and Tevere Valleys was settled by the Etruscans, whose origin (Eastern?) and language (pre-Indo-European) are still unknown. Tuscany, in fact, was named after this mysterious population called Tyrrhenoi *by the Greeks whose territory, known as* Etruria *and* Tuscia *in Latin, became* Toscana *in Italian. The Etruscan city-states (e.g., Florence, Volterra, Populonia, Arezzo, Chiusi and Siena, the main centers) were autonomous entities, united, however, by religious and linguistic bonds. Around the 7th-6th centuries B.C., the territory under Etruscan control extended as far as the Po Valley plains and Corsica. In the 5th century, after being soundly beaten by the Greeks and Carthaginians, the Etruscans were compelled to give up their newly-acquired dominions and retreat within their original borders. Then in the 4th century, subjugated by Rome, they disappeared forever. Despite completion of a host of public works (great roads such as the Aurelia and Cassia, aqueducts, and similar undertakings), Tuscany did not prosper in the Roman era. In the Early Middle Ages, it became a Longobard duchy, but, aside from Lucca which retained a certain degree of importance, the other Tuscan cities were soon reduced to little more than provincial villages. Under Frankish rule, when feudalism and monasticism became increasingly widespread, there was slight improvement,* but not until the 12th century can we speak of full-fledged economic and political reawakening. During the 12th century, in fact, Pisa, facilitated by the Crusades, established intensive trade relations with the Orient, and Florence and Siena embarked on equally intense industrial (textiles) and financial (banking) activities. In the course of the 1100s the emerging bourgeoise found itself at odds with the establishment of the day, i.e., the feudal lords and emperor, and the first contrasts arose among the Tuscan cities. This led to internecine squabbles which eventually resulted (12th century) in the supremacy of Guelph Florence (backed by the Pope and the Anjous) over the pro-Ghibelline centers such as Siena. Tuscany prospered up until the mid 1200s when a succession of setbacks (famine, plague, and financial crises) wrought havoc on the Florentine and Sienese economies. Revolts by the lower classes (of which the most famous was the 1378 Ciompi uprising) failed to undermine Florence's position as the leading Tuscan city. In fact, by the early 1400s, only two cities, Lucca and Siena, were not under Florentine rule (Pisa having been conquered in 1406). In 1436 Florence's ostensibly democratic government fell to the Medicis who would rule the city for the next three centuries. Cosimo the Elder and Lorenzo the Magnificent made the city into the cultural and economic capital of Italy, and the greatest world power of its day. In the 16th century, the Medici Signoria gave way to the Medici grandduchy. Under Grandduke Cosimo I, Siena was subdued, the academies and university were founded, and all the Tuscan cities except for the Republic of Lucca came under Medici rule. Cosimo's successors, however, were

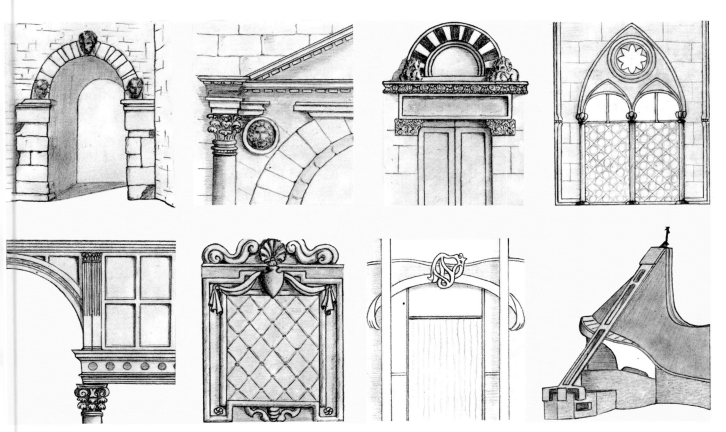

Examples of a number of architectural styles, from top to bottom and from left to right: Etruscan doorway; Roman triumphal arch; Romanesque portal; Gothic mullioned window; Renaissance architecture; Baroque window; Liberty window; Contemporary architecture.

unable to follow in his footsteps and the Tuscan state fell from power, both economically and politically. The last Medici grandduke Gian Gastone died in the middle of the 18th century without leaving any heirs. Thereafter, the Lorraine dynasty gained political control of the region and, especially under the enlightened rule of the great reformer Pietro Leopoldo, brought renewed prosperity and peace. At the turn of the 19th century, Tuscany became part of the French empire, with Lucca as the duchy ruled by Napoleon's sister, Elisa Bonaparte. An active participant in the Risorgimento struggle, the region adhered to the Kingdom of Italy in 1860. By 1815 the Lorraines had returned to power, while Lucca passed into Bourbon hands. Nevertheless, the change from the enlightened rule of the Lorraine to the Savoys' heavier hand was frought with difficulties, especially at the outset. Soon after, however, Tuscany, like the other advanced regions of Italy, embarked on a period of industrialization and great cultural activity. Economically depressed between the two world wars, it has been enjoying a boom ever since the early years of the postwar period, especially in tourism and manufacturing (e.g., textiles in Prato, papermaking in Lucca, heavy industry in Pistoia and Florence, as well as chemicals, shipbuilding, and mining elsewhere).

ART

Most of the manifestations of Etruscan art that have survived in Tuscany (tombs and tomb fittings) come from the great Etruscan cities (i.e., Volterra, Chiusi, Fiesole, Vetulonia, Cortona, and Populonia) which reached their greatest splendor between the 7th and 5th centuries B.C. Dating from this period are the typically Etruscan bucchero vases (made of a special type of terracotta), funerary urns of terracotta or alabaster, and jewelry. On the other hand, few Roman remains aside from the Luni and Arezzo amphitheaters, the Fiesole theater, and some villas, have survived. Artistic activity flourished once more in the Romanesque period (11th-12th centuries) when the great basilicas and tiny country churches (pievi) were built and then adorned outside (portal sculpture) and inside (frescoes and sculpture). The styles born in Pisa and Florence influenced art and architecture throughout their respective spheres of influence. In terms of civic architecture, tower houses commissioned by the emerging merchant class were built inside the city walls of Florence, Lucca, and San Gimignano, whereas great castles dominated the outlying territories. In the 13th century, a new style born from the mixture of Northern European Gothic with local Romanesque produced numerous architectural masterpieces including Florence's Palazzo Vecchio, Siena's Palazzo Pubblico, and Pisa's Camposanto. The foremost artists of the period were Arnolfo di Cambio, architect, Giovanni Pisano, sculptor, and Giotto di Bondone, painter. Their contemporary was Dante Alighieri, who wrote the Divine Comedy at the turn of the 13th

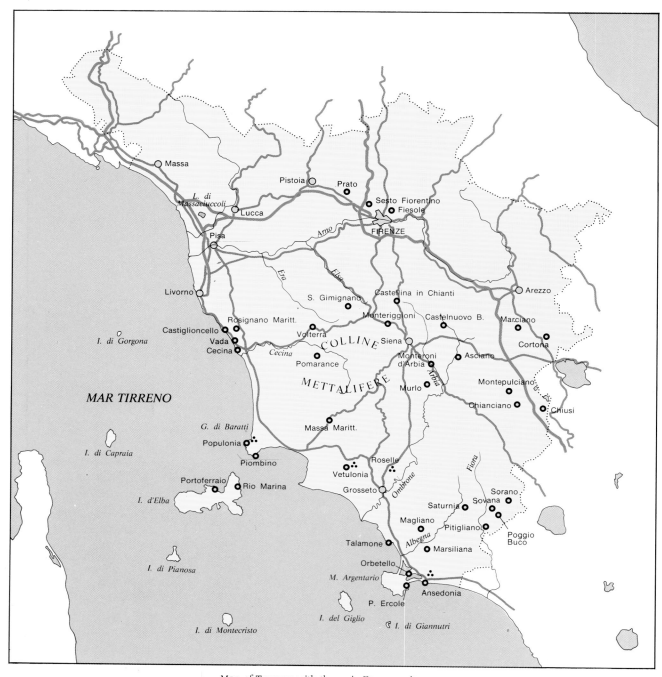

Map of Tuscany with the main Etruscan sites.

century. The only painting school able to challenge Florence's supremacy in the 13th-14th centuries was Siena's represented by Simone Martini and the Lorenzetti brothers. In the 15th century, the so-called Early. Renaissance period, a host of works of the most remarkable originality were produced in Florence: Brunelleschi designed the dome of the Cathedral and Palazzo Pitti, Leon Battista Alberti devised a new set of architectural precepts, Ghiberti cast the great doors of the Florentine Baptistry, Donatello produced remarkable sculptures of saints and heroes. In painting, Masaccio, Paolo Uccello, and Fra Angelico (among others) further developed Giotto's innovative use of perspective and space. The Renaissance artists strived to reach a harmonious naturalistic style based on

perspective, foreshortening, and scientific treatment of light and shade. Originating in Florence, this great cultural debate not only spread throughout Tuscany and Italy, but soon affected the art and culture of the whole world, especially in the 15th and 16th centuries when artists of the ilk of the Lippis, Botticelli, Leonardo and Michelangelo were active in the great Medici courts. The late 16th century was dominated by the intellectual Mannerists, the most famous of which were Bronzino, Pontormo, Rosso Fiorentino, and Vasari. Although Tuscany's artistic output declined in the 17th-18th centuries, the region once more became an artistic center in the 19th century with the birth of the «Macchiaiolo» movement somewhat akin to French Impressionism.

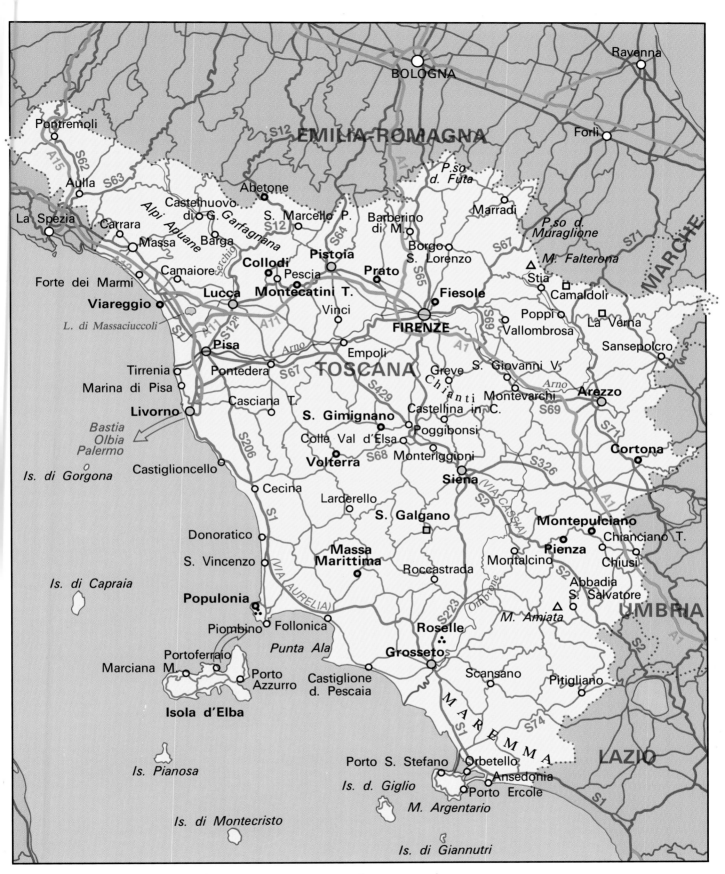

Map of Tuscany.

FLORENCE

Florence, dubbed «cradle of the Renaissance», «Athens of Italy», and just plain Firenze in Italian, was for over a thousand years a quiet town in the Tuscan countryside. Settled by the Etruscans, a Roman encampment, and then a domain of the Holy Roman Empire, its political and economic rise only began around the 11th-12th centuries when, despite warring between the Guelph and Ghibelline factions and recurrent revolts of the populace, prosperity from trade laid the way for its future leadership position. In fact, by the 12th century, when it was a city-state and the first guilds (the famous *Corporazioni delle Arti*) were already functioning, the Florentine *fiorino* had become one of the strongest currencies in all of Europe. In the 13th century, the city's prosperity increased even more. This was the century dominated by Dante Alighieri, whose *Divina Commedia* written in the language spoken by the Florentines and not erudite Latin, laid the basis for modern Italian. In painting Giotto and in architecture Arnolfo di Cambio made their remarkable contributions. In the 14th century, a time of combined economic hardship and plague (the Black Death of 1348 chronicled by Boccaccio in *Decameron*), Northern Gothic, known in painting as the International Style, was the strongest influence on the major Florentine artists, most of whom followers of Giotto. In 1434 with the fall of the Communal form of government, Cosimo de' Medici, known as the Elder, seized power, thereby giving rise to what would be three centuries of Medici rule. By the second half of the century, the Renaissance (literally, rebirth) was well underway, as Cosimo's grandson, Lorenzo the Magnificent, presided over a remarkable court imbued with Classical inspired Humanist culture. Under the patronage of the great Renaissance prince, the arts flourished as few times before (and after) in the history of mankind, producing names such as Lorenzo himself, Poliziano, and Pulci in literature, Botticelli, the Lippis, Ghirlandaio, and Paolo Uccello, in painting, Brunelleschi, Michelozzo, and Alberti in architecture, and Donatello, Verrocchio, and the della Robbias in sculpture. Lorenzo was also a clever politician, managing to attain a correct balance of power among the major contenders of his day, but his successors failed to live up to his greatness, with the result that the Medicis were driven from the city in the late 1400s and the citizenry proclaimed the Republic of Florence. Shortly afterward, however, the Medici triumphantly returned. Cosimo I, the first Medici grandduke, skillfully consolidated Florence's dominions in Tuscan territory, without relinquishing the great tradition of art patronage started by his predecessors. He was succeeded by Francesco I, also a notable art patron, one of whose projects was founding of the Uffizi collection. The Medici and their successors, the Lorraine granddukes, continued to promote artistic endeavors of every sort, commissioning great villas and monumental palaces for themselves, although the political importance of Florence had in the meantime greatly declined. The outstanding events of the 19th century were the Risorgimento struggle and Florence's brief period as the capital of the newly established Kingdom of Italy (1865-1871). No longer a political capital, the city has nevertheless maintained its standing as great cultural and artistic capital. It is renowned all over the world not only for its art masterpieces, but also for its shopping delights, gourmet cooking, and great wines. The major events are the *Scoppio del Carro* (literally, explosion of the cart, held on Easter Sunday), *Calcio in Costume*, forerunner of modern-day soccer, played in 16th century dress (May and June games), and the *Maggio Musicale* (May through June).

RECOMMENDED ITINERARIES – Despite the fact that there's so much to see in Florence, most of the sights are concentrated in the old section where strolling

Above: the «Scoppio» (Explosion) of the Easter Cart; below: the banner-wavers of the Football in Costume («Calcio in Costume»).

Above: view of Florence from Piazzale Michelangelo; below: Dante and the Divine Comedy, by Domenico di Michelino, in the Cathedral of Florence; left: a number of crests of the main Corporations of the Arts and Trades.

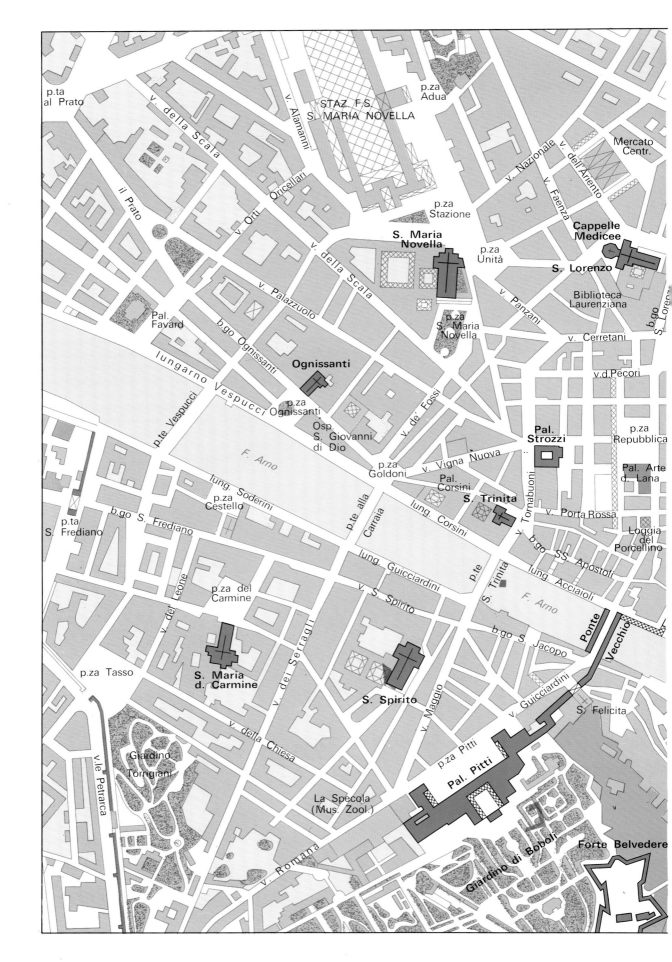

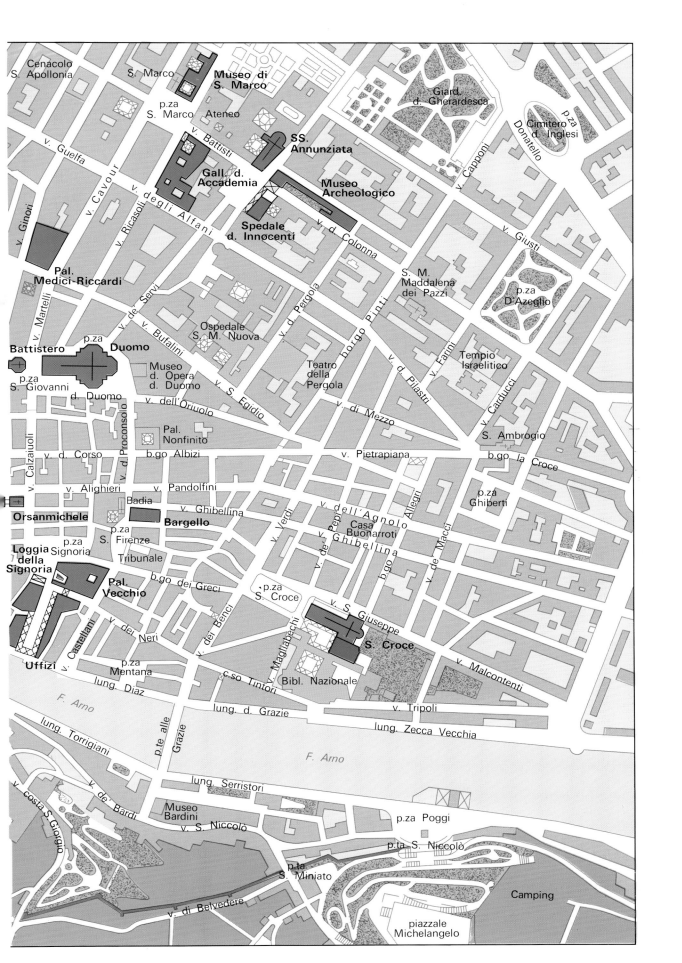

Cenacolo
S. Apollonia
S. Marco
Museo di
S. Marco
p.za
S. Marco
Ateneo
Giard.
d. Gherardesca
p.za
Cimitero
d. Inglesi
Donatello
v. Guelfa
v. Battisti
SS.
Annunziata
v. Cavour
Gall. d.
Accademia
Museo
Archeologico
v. Capponi
v. Ginori
v. Ricasoli
v. degli Alfani
Spedale
d. Innocenti
v. d. Colonna
v. d. Pergola
S. M.
Maddalena
dei Pazzi
v. Giusti
Pal.
Medici-Riccardi
v. de' Servi
borgo Pinti
p.za
D'Azeglio
v. Martelli
v. Bufalini
Ospedale
S. M. Nuova
v. d. Pilastri
v. Farini
Tempio
Israelitico
Battistero
p.za
Duomo
Museo
d. Opera
d. Duomo
Teatro
della
Pergola
v. Carducci
p.za
S. Giovanni
d. Duomo
v. S. Egidio
v. di Mezzo
S. Ambrogio
v. dell'Oriuolo
v. Calzaiuoli
v. d. Proconsolo
Pal.
Nonfinito
b.go Albizi
v. Pietrapiana
b.go la Croce
v. d. Corso
v. Alighieri
v. Pandolfini
p.za
Ghiberti
Badia
v. Ghibellina
v. dell'Agnolo
Allegri
Orsanmichele
Bargello
v. Verdi
v. de' Pepi
Casa
Buonarroti
Ghibellina
v. de' Macci
p.za
S. Firenze
b.go
Loggia
della
Signoria
p.za
Signoria
Tribunale
b.go dei Greci
p.za
S. Croce
v. S. Giuseppe
Pal.
Vecchio
v. dei Neri
v. dei Benci
Magliabechi
S. Croce
v. Malcontenti
Uffizi
v. Castellani
p.za
Mentana
c.so Tintori
Bibl. Nazionale
lung. Diaz
lung. d. Grazie
v. Tripoli
F. Arno
p.te alle Grazie
lung. Zecca Vecchia
lung. Torrigiani
F. Arno
lung. Serristori
v. de' Bardi
Museo
Bardini
p.za Poggi
v. costa S. Giorgio
v. S. Niccolò
p.ta S. Niccolò
p.ta
S. Miniato
Camping
v. di Belvedere
piazzale
Michelangelo

the historic streets is part of the pleasure. Consequently, except for Itinerary 6, the following are all walking tours. Itinerary 6, on the other hand, which entails a panoramic drive, requires a car or city bus ride.

1st ITINERARY: After touring the remarkable sights in *Piazza del Duomo* (**Cathedral**, **Baptistry**, **Giotto's Belltower**, **Cathedral Museum**), proceed the whole length of one of the major shopping streets leading off it, *Via Calzaiuoli*, stopping midway for a visit to the **Orsanmichele** church. Via Calzaiuoli comes out in **Piazza Signoria** featuring another cluster of outstanding monuments (**Palazzo Vecchio**, **Loggia della Signoria**, **Uffizi Gallery**).

2nd ITINERARY: From the *Piazza San Giovanni* side of Piazza del Duomo, take *Via Roma*, another elegant shopping street. Cross *Piazza della Repubblica* with its renowned coffee houses and open-air cafés to Via Calimala which leads to the **Straw Market** (*Loggia del Porcellino*). Then, proceed down Via Por Santa Maria to **Ponte Vecchio**, cross it, and continue down Via Guicciardini until you reach **Palazzo Pitti** whose sights include several museums and the **Boboli Gardens**. A street opposite the palace, Sdrucciolo de' Pitti, leads to **Santo Spirito**. From the square take Via Sant'Agostino and then Via Santa Monica to reach the **Carmine Church** in the heart of *San Frediano*, one of the famous historic districts of Florence.

3rd ITINERARY: Take **Via del Proconsolo** (off Piazza del Duomo, north side of the cathedral apse). On the left you pass Buontalenti's *Palazzo Nonfinito* (16th century) and Giuliano da Maiano's *Palazzo Pazzi* (15th century), while on the right are two major monuments: the **Bargello** (**National Museum**) on the left and the **Badia** on the right. Via Proconsolo comes out in *Piazza San Firenze*: the Baroque facade of the *Courthouse* is on the left and Sangallo's *Palazzo Gondi* (1494) is on the right. Turn left into Borgo dei Greci, a narrow street that leads into **Piazza Santa Croce**. Nearby is the *Biblioteca Nazionale* one of the most important libraries in Italy.

4th ITINERARY: Take *Via Martelli* from Piazza del Duomo (facade side). Turn left on Via dei Gori to reach **San Lorenzo** (church and marketplace) and the **Medici Chapels**, or go straight to *Piazza San Marco*. (Along the way are fine palaces, including the renowned **Palazzo Medici-Riccardi** at the corner of Via Martelli and *Via Cavour*). On the square are several notable sights: the church of *San Marco*, the **San Marco Museum**, the *University of Florence campus*, and the **Accademia** (entrance on Via Ricasoli). Take Via Battisti to Piazza **Santissima Annunziata** (church and **Spedale degli Innocenti**) and continue to Via della Colonna (**Museo Archeologico**).

5th ITINERARY: Not far from the *Santa Maria Novella Station* (designed by Giovanni Michelucci in 1935) is the church of **Santa Maria Novella** on the square of the same name. From Piazza Stazione, take *Via Panzani*, turning right into Via Rondinelli which continues as **Via Tornabuoni**. Along the way to the river are **Palazzo Strozzi** and the church of **Santa Trinita**. Cross *Ponte Santa Trinita*, take *Lungarno Guicciardini* on the right up to the next bridge, *Ponte alla Carraia*, and cross back to *Piazza Goldoni*. Here, making a left you come to the church of *Ognissanti*, while going right into Via della Vigna Nuova you soon reach *Palazzo Rucellai*, a famous Early Renaissance palace designed by Leon Battista Alberti and Bernardo Rossellino.

6th ITINERARY: The scenic drive, *Viale Michelangelo* starts from Piazza Ferrucci on the left bank of the Arno. After stopping at **Piazzale Michelangelo** and the church of **San Miniato al Monte**, continue along *Viale Galileo* to *Via San Leonardo*, which winds its charming way to 16th century *Forte Belvedere*, in a superb panoramic setting.

1st ITINERARY

CATHEDRAL – When the old church of *Santa Reparata* (c. 4th-5th century) could no longer contain Florence's growing Christian community, Arnolfo di Cambio was commissioned to design a cathedral to be built right over it (1289). After his death in 1302, it was continued by artists of great renown such as Giotto, Andrea Pisano, and Brunelleschi. The facade, having been erected in the 19th century, does not belong to the original project.

Brunelleschi worked on the remarkable dome from the 1420s to 1434. Of note are the cathedral's lateral portals: the early 15th century *Porta della Mandorla* (north side) and the 14th century *Porta dei Canonici* (south side). The feeling of stark majesty pervading the *interior* is enhanced by the oversize pillars and impressive stained *glass windows* (14th-15th century). On the left wall are two celebrated frescoes commemorating 15th century military figures: *John Hawk-*

Interior of the Cathedral; below: detail of the mosaics on the dome of the Baptistery.

Aerial view of the Cathedral, with Giotto's Bell Tower and the Baptistery of St. John; below: the Baptistery; the Cathedral and the Bell Tower.

wood painted by Paolo Uccello in 1436 alongside the chiaroscuro *Niccolò da Tolentino* painted by Andrea del Castagno in 1456. On the same side some feet beyond is a panel depicting *Dante and his Divine Comedy* by Domenico di Michelino (1465). A *Crucifix* by Benedetto da Maiano dated 1497 adorns the main altar. The dome is covered by the world's largest fresco, an impressive *Last Judgment* by Vasari, Zuccari, and helpers. A flight of stairs in the right aisle leads down to the *Crypt of Santa Reparata* which not only contains remains of the original Florentine cathedral (architecture, fragments, carved tombs, and frescoes), but also the recently-discovered tomb of the great Brunelleschi.

BAPTISTRY – Probably built around the 5th century, the Baptistry is a striking eight-sided green and white marble building. The sculpted *doors* on three sides are celebrated works: on the south, *scenes from the life of St. John the Baptist* by Andrea Pisano (1330), on the north, *scenes from the New Testament* by Ghiberti (1401), and, on the east, one of the great masterpieces of Early Renaissance art, the *Gates of Paradise* (as Michelangelo reputedly described them), sculpted with *Old Testament stories* by Ghiberti (1425-1452). The *mosaics* adorning the interior (some of which attributed to Cimabue) date from the 1200s.

GIOTTO'S BELLTOWER – Giotto started work on the stunning green and white belltower in 1334, although the project was completed after his death in by Andrea Pisano and Francesco Talenti. Some of the *reliefs* on the base of the building (copies, the originals are in the Museo dell'Opera del Duomo) while sculpted by Andrea Pisano are believed to have been designed by Giotto himself. The view from the 85-meter-tall tower is well worth the climb.

CATHEDRAL MUSEUM – The museum (located on the northeast side of Piazza del Duomo) houses works originally part of the nearby religious complex. Its best-known treasure is Michelangelo's dramatic *Pietà*. Left unfinished, the group waa sculpted around 1550 for the master's own tomb. Other highlights include sculpture by Arnolfo, Donatello, and Nanni di Banco (from the original Cathedral facade), the two Cathedral *Cantorie* (one sculpted by Luca della Robbia in 1438 and one by Donatello in 1455), Donatello's wooden *Mary Magdalene* carved in 1455 for the Baptistry, Andrea Pisano's reliefs for the Belltower (*Labors of Man, Creation of Adam and Eve*, the *Planets*, and the *Liberal Arts*), as well as reliquaries, vestments, and a 15th century *altar frontal* crafted by celebrated artists among whom Verrocchio, Pollaiolo, and Michelozzo.

ORSANMICHELE – The original building that Arnolfo erected in 1290 on the site of the church of San Michele in Orto as a covered trade center for the local wheat dealers was rebuilt in the 14th century after being totally destroyed by fire. The new structure with its great arches and tracery windows is typically Gothic in style. In the niches around the outside are 14th-15th century statues of the *Patron Saints of the Guilds* that commissioned them from the great artists of the day, e.g., Donatello, Nanni di Banco, Ghiberti, and Verrocchio. Inside the striking church interior, adorned with frescoes, sculpture, and stained glass windows, is Orcagna's celebrated *Tabernacle of the Madonna delle Grazie* (1359) which contains a painting of the *Virgin by* Bernardo Daddi. The upstairs may be reached from the neighboring 14th century palace (the *Palazzo dell'Arte della Lana*) to which the church is joined by an overhead walkway.

PIAZZA DELLA SIGNORIA – From the early 1400s to this day, the square has been the scene of the major Florentine political events. A plaque, for example, marks the spot where the reformer monk Savonarola was burned at the stake in 1498. The south side of the square is dominated by the three great arches of the *Loggia della Signoria* (which is also known by two other names: *Loggia dei Lanzi* because the Medicis' Swiss guards, the *Lanzichenecchi*, used to station under it in the 16th century and *Loggia dell'Orcagna* because it was

Giotto's Bell Tower; below: the apse of the Cathedral.

A section of Via Calzaioli, with the great square bulk of Orsanmichele abutting onto it; below: the «Pietà» (Deposition), Michelangelo's masterpiece in the Museum of the Cathedral (Museo dell'Opera del Duomo).

The Paradise Doors, by Lorenzo Ghiberti; below: the Choir-loft Room in the Museum of the Cathedral (Museo dell'Opera del Duomo).

The Neptune Fountain, by Bartolommeo Ammannati; below: the Loggia de' Lanzi in an old painting.
Opposite: Piazza della Signoria.

once erroneously attributed to Orcagna.) Designed in the 1380s by Benci di Cione and Simone Talenti for public ceremonies, it became an open-air sculpture museum as great works such as Benvenuto Cellini's *Perseus* (1554) and Giambologna's *Rape of the Sabine Women* (1583) were set up inside it. The *Neptune Fountain* in front of Palazzo Vecchio is composed of an immense statue representing *Neptune* sculpted by Ammannati and statues of *seagods* and *seahorses* by Giambologna. Giambologna also sculpted the nearby *equestrian statue of Cosimo I dei Medici* (1594). Across the way is the **Alberto della Ragione Collection** of Italian Modern Art.

PALAZZO VECCHIO – Arnolfo designed the building in 1299 and its *tower* in 1310, although modifications were made in the 14th-15th centuries and in the 16th by Vasari and Buontalenti. The distinctive crenelated building with its rusticated stone facing and asymmetrical tower was a symbol of the Free Commune of Florence whose headquarters it was during the Middle Ages, even when it thereafter belonged to those who toppled the Commune, the Medicis. From 1865 to 1872 the Italian Chamber of Deputies, it is now Florence's city hall. The emblems below the crenelation represent the Tuscan cities, while atop the 16th century portal is the symbol of Christ the king. The statues in front are (left to right): the *Marzocco lion* by Donatello (copy), *David* by Michelangelo (copy), and *Hercules and Cacus* by Bandinelli.

The main *courtyard* designed by Michelozzo (15th century) was frescoed and stuccoed by Vasari (16th century). The *putto* adorning the *fountain* is a copy of Verrocchio's 1476 original. The immense *Salone dei Cinquecento* (Hall of the 500), designed by Cronaca in 1495, was decorated by Vasari around the mid-1500s. On the south end is Michelangelo's statue of *Victory* (1534). Off the hall is the *Studiolo* of Francesco I. Designed by Vasari and the Humanist scholar Borghini in 1572 for Francesco's collections, it was decorated by the foremost Mannerist artists of the 16th century. On the same floor, are the *Quartiere del Mezzanino* by Michelozzo now a small art museum, the *Loeser Collection*, featuring 14th-16th century Tuscan painting and sculpture) and the *Sala dei Duecento* (Hall of the 200) designed by the da Maianos. On the third floor are the Medici apartments: the *Quartiere di Eleonora di Toledo* (Cosimo I's wife) designed by Vasari, with a notable *chapel* decorated by Bronzino; the *Quartiere degli Elementi*, again by Vasari; the striking *Sala dei Gigli* with a carved portal by Benedetto da Maiano, frescoes (including one by Ghirlandaio dated 1485), and a coffered ceiling by Giuliano da Maiano. The *Cancelleria* was Machiavelli's office in the 15th century.

GALLERIA DEGLI UFFIZI – The building was commissioned in the 1560s by Cosimo I as offices (*uffizi*) from which to administer the affairs of state of his domain, the Grandduchy of Tuscany. Vasari, the architect picked by Cosimo, came up with a striking design consisting of two porticoed wings joined by a great archway on the river side. A few years later he completed a second project, this one in record time: the Corridoio Vasariano which runs from the Uffizi, crosses the river, and ends a half a kilometer away at Palazzo Pitti. The building was turned into an art gallery by Bernardo Buontalenti in 1582 who received the commission from Cosimo's successor Francesco I. Buontalenti not only reorganized the rooms, but also added some new elements, e.g., the striking Tribuna. The collection, enriched over the years by Francesco's successors, became property of the state in 1743 when the last of the Medicis, Anna Maria Ludovica, left it to the City of Florence.

On the ground floor are two halls once part of *San Pietro Scheraggio*, the Romanesque church that Vasari incorporated into the Uffizi. Andrea del Castagno's celebrated frescoes of *Famous Men*, painted around 1450, are displayed in the first. Midway up the *Scalone Vasariano* is the **Gabinetto dei Disegni e delle Stampe**, the prints and drawings room. The collection, begun in the 17th century, includes works by Paolo Uccello, Leonardo, Michelangelo, and Rubens. The painting gallery is laid out U-fashion, i.e., the exhibition halls radiate off three *corridors* which in themselves are exhibition halls (with Greek and Roman sculpture, 16th century tapestries, a series of portraits, and ceilings frescoed with grotesque designs, as well as lovely views). Room I: Greek and Roman sculpture. Room II: 13th-14th century Tuscan school: Cimabue's *Virgin*

PALAZZO DELLA SIGNORIA - Judith and Holophernes, the magnificent bronze statue by Donatello, after its recent restoration; below: Hercules and Diomedes, by Vincenzo de' Rossi.

The Hall of the Five Hundred, in Palazzo della Signoria; below: the Loggia of the Uffizi, an old print at the Museum of Florence as it was (Firenze com'era).

THE UFFIZI GALLERY - Allegory of Spring, by Sandro Botticelli; below: Annunciation, by Simone Martini and Lippo Memmi; Portrait of Battista Sforza, by Piero della Francesca.

THE UFFIZI GALLERY - The Birth of Venus, by Sandro Botticelli; below: Portrait of Federico da Montefeltro, by Piero della Francesca; Holy Family, by Michelangelo known as the Doni Tondo.

Enthroned (c. 1280), Duccio's *Maestà* (1285), and Giotto's *Maestà* (1310). Room III: 14th century Sienese school: the *Beata Umiltà Altarpiece*, by Pietro Lorenzetti, and the remarkable *Annunciation* painted by Simone Martini and Lippo Memmi (1333). Room IV: 14th century Florentine school. Room V-VI: International Style works, including *The Tebaide* by Starnina, Gentile da Fabriano's *Adoration of the Magi* (1423), and Lorenzo Monaco's immense *Coronation of the Virgin* (c. 1420). Room VII: Fra Angelico paintings, *Virgin and Child with St. Anne* by Masolino and Masaccio (1424), portraits of *Battista Sforza* and *Federico da Montefeltro*, by Piero della Francesca; and Paolo Uccello's renowned *Battle of San Romano* (c. 1456). Room VIII: works by Filippo Lippi, including a celebrated *Virgin and Child*. Room IX: Pollaiolo. Room X-XIV: Botticelli masterpieces: The *Allegory of Spring* (1478), *Birth of Venus* (1486), and *Adoration of the Magi* are displayed, as well as two renowned Northern School paintings, Hugo Van der Goes' *Portinari Altarpiece* and Van der Weyden's *Deposition*. Leonardo Hall: *Baptism of Christ* (mostly by Verrocchio, the blond angel on the left is Leonardo's), *Annunciation*, and the never finished *Adoration of the Magi*. Buontalenti's **Tribuna**, a splendid example of 16th century design, is hung with superb portraits (many of which by Bronzino) and adorned with Classical sculpture and Mantegna paintings. Room XX: German school, including Dürer's *Adoration of the Magi* (1504) and Cranach's panels of *Adam* and *Eve*. Room XXI: Venetians: Giorgione, Carpaccio, and Giovanni Bellini's enigmatic *Allegory*. Room XXII: Holbein and Altdorfer. Room XXIII: Correggio. Room XXV: Michelangelo's only canvas painting, the *Doni Tondo* (1504) and Rosso Fiorentino's *Moses Defending the Daughters of Jethro*, Room XXVI: *Madonna delle Arpie*, by the Mannerist, Andrea del Sarto, and two celebrated Raphaels: the *Virgin of the Goldfinch* (1506) and *portrait of Leo X*. Room XXVII: Pontormo's *Supper in the House of Emmaus*. Room XXVIII. Remarkable Titians, including the sensual *Venus of Urbino* (1538), *Flora*, and *portrait of Eleonora Gonzaga*. Room XXIX: Parmigianino's *Virgin with the Long Neck*. Room XXXI: bizarre subject paintings by Dosso Dossi. Room XXXII: 16th century Venetian School. Room XXXIV: *Holy Family with St. Barbara*, by Veronese and *portrait of Count Secco-Suardo*, by Moroni. Room XLI: masterpieces by Rubens, including the immense *Henry IV's Entry into Paris* (1628) and the striking *portrait of Isabel Brandt*; portraits by Van Dyck and Sustermans. Niobe Room: Temporary exhibitions are held in this room adorned with Roman copies of 3rd century B.C. Hellenistic statues representing *Niobe and her daughters*. Room XLIII: Caravaggio's *Bacchus*, *Medusa* shield, and dramatic *Sacrifice of Isaac* (c. 1590), Annibale Carracci's *Baccanal*, and a *seascape* by Claude Lorrain. Room XLIV: Goya, Canaletto, Carriera, Longhi, Chardin, Tiepolo. The great raised passageway known as the **Corridoio Vasariano** is entered from the third (west) corridor of the gallery. It is hung with Caravaggio school paintings and a celebrated collection of *self-portraits* (Leonardo, Titian, Dürer, Rubens, Veronese, Velazquez, Ingres, Fattori, and Pellizza da Volpedo, among others).

2nd ITINERARY

LOGGIA DEL PORCELLINO (STRAW MARKET) – The loggia was designed by Giovanni Battista del Tasso in 1511 as the gold and silk merchants' trade center. It is now the popular open-air marketplace everyone calls the Straw Market. Originally known as the Loggia di Mercato Nuovo (new market), it was later renamed after the bronze boar (*porcellino*) adorning the fountain on the south of the square.

PONTE VECCHIO – From Antiquity there was always a bridge crossing the Arno at this point, to connect Florence's most populated area with the Via Cassia. Every time one was destroyed by floods, another was built in its place. (This one dates from the 14th century). The jewelry shops lining the bridge replaced the butcher shops banished by Ferdinando I in the late 1500s. The windows along the top belong to the Corridoio Vasariano (see Galleria degli Uffizi).

PALAZZO PITTI – This remarkable palace was designed by Brunelleschi around the mid-1400s for a rival of the Medicis, Luca Pitti. The original building was much smaller (running the length of only the seven central windows). It was remodeled and enlarged in the 16th century as a showplace worthy of its new owners. Another Medici project, landscaping of the immense palace grounds, was carried out by Tribolo. Extensive modifications were also made in the 17th and 18th

THE UFFIZI GALLERY - The Medici Venus, a 3rd century copy of the Greek original; below: Fountain known as the «Porcellino» (Little Pig), a bronze copy by Pietro Tacca, of the Hellenistic original marble boar in the Uffizi Gallery.

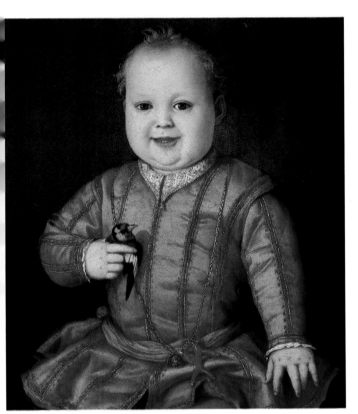

THE UFFIZI GALLERY - Don Garzia de' Medici and Eleonora of Toledo, two portraits, by Agnolo Bronzino; below: view of the Arno river, with the Ponte Vecchio in the foreground.

PITTI PALACE - The façade; below: the Mars Room.

THE PALATINE GALLERY - The Consequences of War, by Pieter Paul Rubens; below: the Expectant Mother and the Veiled Lady, both by Raphael.

centuries. Today the palace is a museum, or rather complex of museums: the **Palatine Gallery**, the **Monumental Apartments**, the **Gallery of Modern Art**, the **Silver Museum**, the **Porcelain Museum**, the **Museum of Costumes** and the **Coach Museum**.

Use the main entrance in the middle of the building, which takes you into Ammannati's imposing *courtyard*. A staircase under the arcading on the righthand side leads to the **Palatine Gallery** on the second floor. One of the major galleries of European painting in existence, it consists of twenty-five rooms lavishly adorned with frescoes by Pietro da Cortona and Ciro Ferri, stucco decoration, and antique furniture. We shall mention only the highlights of the rooms named after the subjects of their ceiling frescoes. Venus Room: statue of *Venus* (*Venere Italica* by Canova, 1811); two *seascapes* by Salvator Rosa, *The Concert* (either a late Giorgione, early Titian, or masterpiece by another painter of their Venetian milieu), *Ulysses on the Isle of Pheaces*. Apollo Room: *portraits of Charles I of England and his wife*, by Van Dyck, *Mary Magdalene* and portrait of a gentleman known as *Man with a Glove* by Titian, Andrea del Sarto's *Holy Family* (1529), and Guido Reni's *Cleopatra* (c. 1640). Mars Room: two famous Rubens: *The Consequences of War* and *The Four Philosophers*, Murillo's delicate Virgin and Child, as well as portraits by Van Dyck, Veronese, Titian. Jupiter Room: the *Virgin of the Sack*, by Perugino, *Deposition* by Bartolomeo (1516), an elegant portrait by Bronzino, *Guidobaldo della Rovere*, and the superb Raphael portrait, *La Velata* (c. 1516), which is believed to be of his mistress. Saturn Room: some of Raphael's best-known masterpieces: *portraits of Maddalena and Agnolo Doni*, the *Madonna del Granduca* (1504), *portrait of Tommaso Inghirami*, and the *Madonna della Seggiola* (*Virgin of the Chair*), painted around 1516, as well as Perugino's *Mary Magdalene* and paintings by Sebastaino del Piombo and Carlo Dolci. Iliad Room: *portrait of Philip IV*, by Velasquez, paintings by Sustermans including *portrait of Christian of Denmark*, Veronese's *Baptism of Christ*, a Caravaggesque rendition of the Biblical heroine *Judith* by Artemisia Gentileschi. Room of the Education of Jupiter: Caravaggio's *Sleeping Cupid* and Cristofano Allori's *Judith*. Ulysses Room: Raphael's *Madonna dell'Impannata*. Prometheus Room: Pontormo's striking *Martyrdom of the 11,000*, Botticelli's *Bella Simonetta*, and Filippo Lippi's *Virgin and Child*. Corridoio delle Colonne: Dutch landscapists, among them Van Poelenburg. Justice Room: Venetian masters (Titian and Tintoretto). Flora Room: Andrea del Sarto and the Florentine Mannerists. Putti Room: Rachel Ruysch's *Flowers and Fruit* and Schalken's *Girl with a Candle*. Galleria Poccetti: Furini's *Ila and the Nymphs*, Feti's *Lost Drachma*, as well as portraits by Rubens and Lely. Allegory Room: Volterrano and Giovanni San Giovanni (17th century). The following rooms exhibit Tuscan school 16th-17th century paintings, except for the Psyche Room hung with a series of fine Salvator Rosas (Neapolitan school). Now retrace your steps to the Sala delle Nicchie (Niche Room) which is the first of the **Monumental Apartments**, i.e., at various times living quarters of the Medicis, Lorraines, and Savoys. (The king of Italy, Vittorio Emanuele II, occupied them between 1865 to 1871, when Florence was capital of the nation.) The most interesting sights are the Throne Room, the Blue Room, the Yellow Room (hung with Gobelins tapestries), the chapel, the bedroom, and the White Room, the grandiose palace ballroom. The **Gallery of Modern Art**, on the third floor, features Italian 19th-early 20th century art, with a special focus on Tuscan school works. The highlights comprise sculpture by Giovanni Dupré, Cassioli's *Battle of Legnano*, Canova's *Head of Calliope*, and works by the *Macchiaioli* e.g., Lega, Fattori, and Signorini. There are also paintings by Previati and Medardo Rosso, as well as Cabianca's *Morning Prayers* and Corcos' *portrait of Jack la Bolina's daughter*. The **Silver Museum**, situated on the ground floor, has a fabulous collection of Medici and Lorraine heirlooms: jewels, enamels, carved ivories, precious stones, and glassware. The highlights are 18th century Italian and German ebony furniture inlaid with ivory and semiprecious stones (stipi chests, tables, and prayer stools), German carved ivories, jasper and lapis-lazuli vases, goblets, and flasks, the remarkable — and, in truth, somewhat bizarre — jewel collection belonging to Maria Luisa, shell sculptures, as well as Oriental objects. Exit from the palace, cross the great courtyard, and enter the Boboli Gardens from the lefthand wing of the building known as the *Rondò di Bacco*. The **Boboli**, where the **Porcelain Museum** and the **Museum of Costumes** are, is one of the earliest examples of Italian-style landscaping and the forerunner of a host of parks and gardens throughout Italy and Europe. The project, entailing landscaping of acres of hillside, was commissioned by Eleonora da Toledo around the mid-1500s, but continued well into the 18th century. The result is rather complex: there are pools, fountains, statuary, miniature forests, lawns, flowerbeds, greenhouses and even an *amphitheater*. Of special note are a man-made grotto, the *Grotta*

THE PALATINE GALLERY - The Man with the Grey Eyes, by Titian; below: the so-called «Bacchino» Fountain, by Cioli. at the entrance of the Boboli Gardens.

THE PALATINE GALLERY - The Madonna of the Chair, by Raphael; the Young Bacchus, by Guido Reni; below: the Neptune Pool in the Boboli Gardens.

del Buontalenti (1588), once adorned with Michelangelo's statues of *Slaves* (now in the Accademia), and the *Oceanus Fountain* designed by Giambologna.

SANTO SPIRITO – An Early Renaissance building designed by Brunelleschi in 1444, it was finished by Manetti in 1487. The slightly later belltower (1517) was designed by Baccio d'Agnolo. The interior is a notable example of Brunelleschi's masterful use of space: an effect of harmony and balance is a achieved through the regular succession of spaces marked by the columns sweeping the eye to the focal point of the building, the dome-crowned crossing. Among the masters whose works are hanging in the church are Filippino Lippi, Sansovino, and Rossellino.

To the right of the church building is the *refectory* of the **Monastery of Santo Spirito** with a *Last Supper* frescoed by Orcagna (c. 1360).

SANTA MARIA DEL CARMINE – Founded in the 13th century, it underwent extensive remodeling. Its present appearance dates from the 18th century. The church's claim to fame is the *Brancacci Chapel*, in the right transept, frescoed by Masaccio. Masaccio's master, Masolino, commissioned by a wealthy merchant, Felice Brancacci, began work on the chapel in 1425, but the project was soon taken over by his pupil whose treatment of figures in believable space made the frescoes among the most important to have come out of the Early Renaissance. The scenes by Masaccio are the *Expulsion from Paradise*, *The Tribute Money*, *St. Peter Healing a Lame Man*, and *St. Peter Raising Tabitha from the Dead* (in conjunction with Masolino). The cycle was finished by Filippino Lippi.

3rd ITINERARY

DANTE'S HOUSE – Actually a group of much restored medieval buildings that originally belonged to Dante's family, the *Casa di Dante* is now a museum. The collection comprises mementos of the great poet's life and works, e.g., various editions of the *Divine Comedy*.

BADIA FIORENTINA – Founded in 978, the church was remodeled in 1282 (possibly by Arnolfo), and then restructured in the 17th century. Alongside is a 14th century *belltower*. Among the highlights are a painting by Filippino Lippi, the *Virgin Appearing to St. Bernard* (c. 1485) to the left of the entrance. On the left side of the crossing is the famous 15th century wall tomb carved by Mino da Fiesole for Count Ugo, Marquis of Tuscany, around the year 1000.

BARGELLO – The forbidding castle was built in 1225 as headquarters for the *Capitano del Popolo*, a kind of governor. Thereafter, police headquarters (starting from the 16th century), it also served as a dungeon and the scene of public executions. The bell in its crenelated tower is only rung on occasions of extraordinary importance (e.g., end of World War II and the flood of 1966). A museum since 1859, it vaunts one of the foremost collections in the world of 15th-16th century Tuscan sculpture, della Robbia ceramics, arms and armor, as well as minor arts.

The **National Museum** starts in a *courtyard* filled with 16th century sculpture and emblems of various *podestà* (mayors) who governed the city. This Sala del Trecento off the courtyard features 13th and 14th century sculpture, among which an extraordinary *Virgin and Child* by Tino da Camaino. In the facing Salone del Cinquecento are famous 16th century masterpieces: Michelangelo's *Tondo Pitti*, bust of *Brutus, Drunken Bacchus*, and *Apollo David*, as well as sculpture by Cellini, Sansovino, Ammannati, and Giambologna. Upstairs is another collection of sculpture masterpieces, including Donatello's *St. George* (1416) and his two celebrated *Davids* (one in marble and a bronze one wearing a hat), as well as the reliefs of the *Sacrifice of Isaac* submitted by Ghiberti and Brunelleschi for the north door of the Baptistry (1402). (Ghiberti's delicate rendering won out over Brunelleschi's more dramatic version.) The minor arts collections comprise medieval ivories (Byzantine, French, and German, as well as Italian). The Cappella del Podestà was frescoed by a follower of Giotto. In

The church of Santo Spirito, overlooking its square; below: view of Piazza San Firenze, with the church of San Firenze and the Palace of the Courts of Justice; in the background: the austere-looking Bargello Palace, where the National Museum of Sculpture is.

The façade of Santa Maria del Carmine; the Tribute, Masaccio's masterpiece in the Brancacci Chapel in the Carmine church; below, right: David, by Verrocchio and David by Donatello, two of the magnificent bronzes in the Bargello Museum.

BARGELLO - The Loggia in the courtyard; below: the «Verone» overlooking the courtyard.

the *Paradise scene* on the the end wall is a celebrated *portrait of Dante*. On the third floor is a unique collection of della Robbia *glazed terracottas* (chiefly religious subjects on sky blue grounds), 15th and 16th century creations by Giovanni, Andrea, and Luca della Robbia. The Sala del Verrocchio contains several of the late-15th century Florentine master's most famous works, including his *David* and a bust of a *Lady with a Bouquet*.

SANTA CROCE – This magnificent Franciscan Gothic church was begun around the mid-1200s (according to tradition by Arnolfo di Cambio), although it was not consecrated until 1443. Italy's Westminster Abbey, it vaunts Giotto's remarkable frescoes, as well as the tombs of famous Italians.

The facade is a 19th century imitation of Gothic. In keeping with the Franciscan tradition, the interior is simple and stately. The nave walls, once covered with Giotto frescoes, are lined with tombs and monuments including Vasari's *Tomb of Michelangelo*, Canova's *Monument to Alfieri*, a *Monument to Machiavelli*, as well as the *Tombs of the composer Rossini, the poet Ugo Foscolo* (right aisle), *Galileo, and Ghiberti* (left aisle). The church is a veritable compendium of 15th century sculpture: Benedetto da Maiano' *Pulpit*, Donatello's *Annunciation*, Rossellino's *Tomb of Leonardo Bruni* (right aisle) and Desiderio da Settignano's *Tomb of Carlo Marsuppini* (left aisle). Most of the chapels in the righthand transept and side were frescoed in the 14th century (*Cappella Castellani* and *Cappella Baroncelli* by Gaddi, *Cappella Rinuccini* by Giovanni da Milano). Giotto's famous frescoes adorn two chapels of the east end, *Cappella Peruzzi* and *Cappella Bardi* (1317, *scenes from the life of St. Francis*). In the central *Cappella Maggiore* frescoed by Agnolo Gaddi is a wooden *crucifix* (unknown master). The last chapel on the left, the *Cappella Bardi di Vernio*, was frescoed by Maso di Banco (14th century). Nearby is a *crucifix* by Donatello. In the pleasant *cloister* (entrance to the right of the church) is the *Tomb of Florence Nightingale*. At the far end is Brunelleschi's *Pazzi Chapel*, one of the masterpiece of Early Renaissance architecture (1440s). Off the adjoining Brunelleschi-style cloister is the **Santa Croce Museum** in which, among other works relating to the church, is Cimabue's great *Crucifix*.

4th ITINERARY

SAN LORENZO – The Medicis commissioned Brunelleschi to remodel the original building. The facade, despite plans drawn up by Michelangelo, was never completed. The superb Brunelleschi interior is adorned with notable works, among them two bronze *pulpits* by Donatello (1460s), Rosso Fiorentino's striking *Marriage of the Virgin* (second right altar), a *tabernacle* by Desiderio da Settignano (end of right aisle), and an *Annunciation* by Filippo Lippi (left transept). The *tomb of Giovanni and Piero dei Medici* by Verrocchio (1472) is in the *Old Sacristy*, designed by Brunelleschi and decorated by Donatello.

MEDICI CHAPELS – There are two tomb complexes: the *Princes Chapel*, the grandukes' grandiose burial hall lavishly faced with colored marbles and semiprecious stones, and the *New Sacristy* designed by Michelangelo in 1524. Some of his most celebrated sculpture adorns the tombs (*Day* and *Night* above Giuliano di Nemours, *Dawn* and *Dusk* above Lorenzo di Urbino, and the *Virgin and Child* above Giuliano and Lorenzo the Magnificent).

PALAZZO MEDICI-RICCARDI – A superb example of 15th century Florentine civic architecture, the palace was designed by Michelozzo in the mid-1400s for Cosimo the Elder and later embellished under Lorenzo the Magnificent. Purchased by the Riccardi family in the 17th century, it underwent remodeling and enlargement.

The first floor of the exterior is faced in rough stone, the second in rusticated stone and the top one in planed blocks. Two of the ground floor windows (the corner ones) are traditionally ascribed to Michelangelo. From the courtyard radiate the **Museo Mediceo** (temporary exhibitions) on the left, an attractive *garden* in the center, and the *Chapel* (stairs to the right). Built by Michelozzo, the chapel was frescoed in 1460 by Benozzo Gozzoli with a scene ostensibly showing the *Wise Men on their way to Bethlehem* (actually portraits of the Medicis). Upstairs is the *Gallery*, an impressive hall frescoed by Luca Giordano in 1683.

SANTA CROCE - The Main Altar Chapel frescoed by Agnolo Gaddi.

SANTA CROCE - The interior.

SANTA CROCE - The right aisle, with the Tomb of Michelangelo, designed by Giorgio Vasari; below: the famous Cimabue Crucifix.

The 19th century façade of Santa Croce, by Nicholas Matas; below: the Pazzi Chapel porch, a Renaissance masterpiece, by Filippo Brunelleschi.

The unfinished façade of San Lorenzo; in the background, the dome of the Medici Princes'Chapel; below: the Medici-Riccardi Palace, the prototype of all Florentine Renaissance mansions, by Michelozzo; detail of the Procession of the Magi on their way to Bethlehem, by Benozzo Gozzoli, in the Medici Palace Chapel.

MEDICI CHAPELS - The sumptuous interior of the Princes' Chapel; below: the Tomb of Giuliano de' Medici, duke of Nemours, and the Tomb of Lorenzo, duke of Urbino, Michelangelo's masterpieces in the New Sacristy of San Lorenzo.

SAN MARCO MUSEUM

SAN MARCO MUSEUM – The museum building, the Monastery of San Marco (built by Michelozzo in 1452), was one of the focal points of Florentine culture throughout the Renaissance. Among the famous men who lived here were Fra Angelico, Savonarola, and Fra Bartolomeo.

The main courtyard, the *Chiostro di Sant'Antonino*, is frescoed. (The *St. Dominick at the feet of the Cross* and *Christ with two Dominican monks* are by Fra Angelico.) The great *Crucifixion* scene in the *Chapter Room* opposite the entrance was also frescoed by Fra Angelico. To the left is the *Sala del Lavabo* (literally, washroom) with a fine *altarpiece* by Fra Bartolomeo. Next to it is the main refectory. On the other side of the cloister is the socalled *Ospizio del Pellegrino* (Pilgrims' Lodgings) which features a collection of superb Fra Angelico panel paintings, including the celebrated *Linaioli Altarpiece* (1433), the *Bosco ai Frati Altarpiece* (a late work), the *St. Mark Altarpiece* (c. 1440), the remarkable *Last Judgment* (c. 1430), and smaller panels with *scenes from the life of Christ*. The most striking painting in the room, however, is the *Deposition*, acclaimed Fra Angelico's masterpiece (c. 1435). Upstairs are the monks' spare cells rendered precious by the religious scenes Fra Angelico and his helpers frescoed on the walls between 1439 and 1445. Among the finest: two *Annunciations*, *Noli Me Tangere*, the *Coronation of the Virgin*, and the *Transfiguration*.

ACCADEMIA (ACADEMY GALLERY)

ACCADEMIA (ACADEMY GALLERY) – Established in 1784, the museum features 13th-16th century Florentine school paintings and some of Michelangelo's most famous sculpture.

The main exhibition halls, the *Salone* and *Tribuna* designed by Emilio De Fabris in the late 1800s, host Michelangelo's sculpture. Along the Salone are the four *Slaves*, roughed out masterpieces of enormous vigor, meant for Pope Julius' (never finished) tomb in Rome (c. 1518), *St. Matthew* (c. 1505), the only one of the planned group of apostles ever carved for the Cathedral of Florence, and the *Palestrina Pietà*, a dramatic example of the master's late style. In the Tribuna stands the *David*, an early work of exceptional effect, that needs no introduction. It was commissioned by the Republic of Florence as the symbol of Florentine freedom and set right in front of Palazzo Vecchio, the city's civic center (where it stood until replacement by a copy became necessary for preservation in the 1800s). The rest of the museum focuses on Florentine painting, from the pre-Renaissance through Mannerist periods. So-called "minor works" (even when by name artists), they nevertheless testify to the remarkably high level attained by Florentine art over the centuries. The chief attractions are: 13th century panel paintings by an unknown masters (Maestro della Maddalena) and Pacino di Buonaguida, *Coronation of the Virgin* by Bernardo Daddi, *Pietà* by Giovanni da Milano, *Virgin and Child* by Filippino Lippi, and the *Cassone Adimari*, a 15th century hopechest adorned with a marriage scene set in a clearly recognizable Piazza del Duomo. 15th and 16th century masters such as Perugino (*Visitation*), Botticelli (three *Virgins*, including the famous *Madonna del Mare*), Fra Bartolomeo, Cosimo Rosselli, Botticini, Pontormo, Bronzino, and Lorenzo di Credi are among the several represented.

SANTISSIMA ANNUNZIATA

SANTISSIMA ANNUNZIATA – Built by Michelozzo between 1444 and 1481 on the site of a pre-existing 13th century oratory, the church was completed by Alberti who designed the dome (lined up with the Cathedral's by means of Via dei Servi's straight-edge configuration). The outer portico dates from the 1600s.

Crossing the porch brings you into the *Chiostrino dei Voti*, a 15th century cloister superbly frescoed by 16th century masters of the ilk of Andrea del Sarto, Pontormo, Franciabigio, and others. Among the highlights of the lavish Baroque interior: *Tempietto* by Michelozzo (housing a much venerated 13th century panel painting of the *Virgin Annunciate*), frescoes by Andrea del Castagno (first two lefthand chapels), the choir rotunda by Alberti and Michelozzo, and the *Monument to Orlando dei Medici* by Rossellino (1456). Off the left transept is a 15th century cloister, the *Chiostro dei Morti*.

SPEDALE DEGLI INNOCENTI

SPEDALE DEGLI INNOCENTI – Brunelleschi designed this masterpiece of Early Renaissance architecture in 1419. The harmonious porticoed facade design is repeated in the 16th century building opposite it and in the 17th century porch of the church of Santissima Annunziata. The della Robbia tondos with *babes in swaddling clothes* are a reference to the Spedale's function as a foundling hospital. The

The Library of the Museum of San Marco with the precious illuminated codexes of the 14th and 15th centuries; below: view of Piazza Santissima Annunziata with one of the fountains by Tacca.

GALLERY OF THE ACADEMY - Overall view of the Tribuna with Michelangelo's masterpieces which include the Pietà of Palestrina (Deposition), below and the David, opposite.

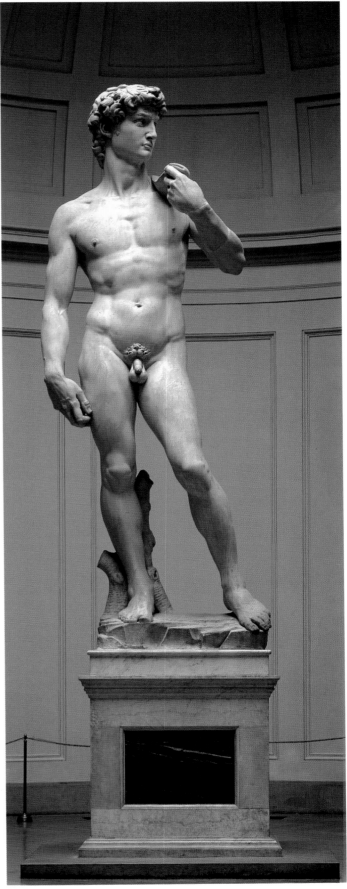

Galleria, the small art museum inside, has a notable collection of 15th-16th century paintings by Botticelli, Ghirlandaio, Piero di Cosimo, and others.

ARCHEOLOGICAL MUSEUM – The museum building is a 17th century palace, *Palazzo della Crocetta*, set in an attractive garden. The collections (established in the late 1800s) comprise Egyptian, Greco-Roman, and Etruscan art, as well as artifacts and coins.

In the ground floor halls are several noteworthy ceramics including the celebrated *François Vase*, a 6th century B.C. Greek black figure vase unearthed by a Frenchman, François, in an Etruscan tomb in Chiusi, as well as Attic and mock Etruscan vases, and Etruscan funerary urns (outstanding of which is the socalled *Mater Matuta*). The highlights of the upstairs **Egyptian Collection** composed mainly of pieces excavated in the 19th century by Rosellini and Schiaparelli are a red basalt *pharoah's bust* (18th century B.C.), a wooden *chariot* from Thebes (14th century B.C.), and two painted *statues of servant girls engaged in household tasks*. The second section, the **Etrusco-Greco-Roman Antiquarium**, features masterpieces of Etruscan art (the *Chimera*, a 5th century mythological creature unearthed in Arezzo, the 3rd century B.C. *Haranger*, a *statue of Minerva*, as well as sarcophagi, urns, and votive statuettes), Greek art (the 5th century B.C. *Idolino* and a Hellenistic *horse's head* which inspired Donatello's horse for the Gattamelata monument in Padua), and Roman sculpture.

5th ITINERARY

SANTA MARIA NOVELLA – Built by Dominican monks in the mid-1200s, the church has a remarkable facade begun in the 14th century and completed by Alberti in the 15th (upper section and portal). The geometric patterns recall the Tuscan-style Romanesque of the 11th-12th centuries (e.g., San Miniato, Baptistry, etc.).

The entranceway to the remarkable *cloisters* is to the left of the facade. The first, the *Chiostro Verde* (c. 1350), is adorned with 15th century frescoes. Next you enter the *Refectory* which Paolo Uccello frescoed around 1430. The most famous scenes are those of the *Flood* and *Sacrifice of Noah*. From the other side of the Chiostro Verde you enter the *Chiostro Grande*, then the *Chiostrino dei Morti*, and finally the *Cappellone degli Spagnoli* or *Spaniards' Chapel*. The Cappellone, built in 1350 and taken over by Eleonora da Toledo's Spanish entourage for their religious services in the 16th century, was superbly frescoed by Andrea di Bonaiuto (c. 1355) with scenes relating to the *history of the Dominican order* and the *life of St. Thomas of Aquinus*. Inside the immense Gothic church are numerous masterpieces of Renaissance art: Masaccio's *Trinity* frescoed around 1427 (left wall), a *Crucifix* by Giotto (in the sacristy off the lefthand aisle), frescoes by Nardo di Cione and an Orcagna altarpiece (*Cappella Strozzi* off the left transept), a celebrated Brunelleschi *Crucifix* (first chapel to the left of the choir), stupendous *scenes from the lives of the Virgin and St. John the Baptist* frescoed by Filippino Lippi (last chapel on the right of the choir), and a tomb carved by Ghiberti along with a *Virgin and Child* by Nino Pisano (*Cappella Rucellai* off the right transept).

VIA TORNABUONI – Lined with famous boutiques as well as superb palaces (including Palazzo Strozzi, described below) it runs from Piazza Antinori to the *Santa Trinita Bridge*. Two notable buildings look out on Piazza Antinori: *Palazzo Antinori*, probably designed by Giuliano da Maiano around 1460, and *San Gaetano*, one of the few Baroque churches in Florence. *Piazza Santa Trinita* at the end of the street is among Florence's loveliest squares. On the right side is the church of Santa Trinita, on the left *Palazzo Bartolini-Salimeni*, an early 16th century Classical style palace designed by Baccio d'Agnolo and *Palazzo Spini-Ferroni* (1289), one of Florence's foremost medieval palaces. In the center is an Egyptian *obelisk* topped by a *statue of Justice*.

PALAZZO STROZZI – Perhaps the most famous example of Renaissance civic architecture, the distinctive palace was commissioned by the Strozzi family and designed by Benedetto da Maiano in 1489. Its great *cornice* and lovely inner *courtyard* were designed by a contemporary of Benedetto's, Cronaca. Today the building is occupied by cultural organizations.

ARCHAEOLOGICAL MUSEUM - The Mater Matuta, an Etruscan funerary statue; below: the interior of Santa Maria Novella.

ARCHAEOLOGICAL MUSEUM - The Chimaera of Arezzo, Etruscan, 5th century B.C. bronze; below: the façade of Santa Maria Novella, by Leon Battista Alberti, dominating the square in front of the church.

SANTA TRINITA – The original building, an 11th century church erected by the Vallombrosan monks, was remodeled in the late 1400s (probably by Neri di Fioravante), while the facade was designed by Buontalenti in the 1590s.

The interior, one of the earliest examples of Florentine Gothic, features outstanding Renaissance works such as a *statue of Mary Magdalene* by Desiderio da Settignano (finished by Benedetto da Maiano in 1465) in the fifth chapel on the left, and a fine *Annunciation* and *scenes from the life of the Virgin* by Lorenzo Monaco on the altar and walls of the fourth righthand chapel. In the *Sassetti Chapel* (far right end) are Ghirlandaio's celebrated frescoes of *scenes from the life of St. Francis* and his *Adoration of the Magi* on the altar.

6th ITINERARY

PIAZZALE MICHELANGELO – With the whole city spread out below your feet, you see, from left to right; the Cascine Park, the dome and immense mass of the Cathedral surrounded by the towers and belltowers of medieval Florence, Santa Croce, with the Arno in the foreground and the Florentine hills in the background. In the center of the square is a copy of the *David* commemorating Michelangelo. Half hidden among the grey-green cypress trees up the hill is the church of **San Salvatore al Monte** designed by Cronaca in 1499.

SAN MINIATO AL MONTE – This superb Romanesque church built between the 11th and 12th centuries features a distinctive green and white patterned marble facade with a superb 13th century mosaic.

The interior has a typically Romanesque plan: single aisles and an east end with a raised choir-lowered crypt arrangement. Of especial note is the 13th century *mosaic floor* of the nave. At the end of the nave is the *Cappella del Crocifisso*, designed by Michelozzo in 1448 and embellished with della Robbia terracottas. Further on is the seven-aisled *crypt* adorned with Taddeo Gaddi frescoes. Above is the choir, surrounded by marble partitions sustaining a pulpit and adorned with an immense 13th century mosaic, 15th century *choir stalls*, and a painting of *St. Miniato* by Jacopo del Casentino. On the right is the *Sacristy* with late 14th century frescoes by Spinello Aretino recounting the life of St. Benedictine. On the left side is the *Cappella del Cardinale del Portogallo*, a Renaissance chapel with the cardinal's *tomb* by Rossellino and an *Annunciation* by Alesso Baldovinetti. In the adjoining *cemetery* is the *Tomb of Carlo Collodi,* the author of *Pinocchio* (1825-1890).

View from the Ponte Santa Trinita down Via Tornabuoni, with the Column of Justice, in the middle of Piazza Santa Trinita, in the background; below: the elegant bulk of Palazzo Strozzi, one of the most splendid examples of Renaissance architecture, by Benedetto da Maiano and Cronaca.

View of Florence from Piazzale Michelangelo; the Monument to Michelangelo, comprising bronze copies of some of the artist's most significant works, in the foreground; below: the interior and exterior of San Miniato al Monte, a magnificent Romanesque church of the 11th-12th centuries.

THE SURROUNDINGS OF FLORENCE

1. Fiesole, Settignano — 2. Pratolino, Montesenario — 3. Castello, Sesto Fiorentino — 4. Certosa del Galluzzo.

1. FIESOLE, SETTIGNANO

From Piazza Edison, one proceeds along Via San Domenico which winds up through gardens and villas to Fiesole, offering delightful views of the hilly landscape on either side. About halfway up the hill, one comes to the hamlet of **San Domenico**, which surrounds the monastery of the same name, which Fra Angelico lived in in the 15th century. There is a *Holy Conversation* by this Florentine master in the church of monastery. From the square in front of the church a road branches off left towards the **Badia Fiesolana**, overlooking the Mugnone valley. The church of the abbey (the monastery buildings are now occupied by the European University) still possesses its magnificent 12th century marble façade. Returning to Via San Domenico and continuing uphill, one encounters the magnificent **Villa Medici** to the left of the road, just before entering Fiesole. The villa was designed by Michelozzo for Cosimo the Elder between 1458 and 1461 and was subsequently much used by the Magnificent Lorenzo and his court of humanists.

FIESOLE – Always a charming and much visited locality it owes most of its popularity to its proximity to Florence, to the balmy climate and enchanting landscape and to the numerous reminders of its glorious Etruscan and Roman past as well of its fascinating Medieval period.

It used to be a very important Etruscan town (its acropolis used to be on the hill known nowadays as San Francesco), which took arms against Rome and was punitively conquered by Silla in 80 B.C. The town continued to grow in the Roman era (the Theatre and Baths) and throughout the early Medieval period, thereafter its fortunes declined as those of Florence grew. Too near and too powerful, the town in the plain overran and conquered the ancient hill-town in 1125, depriving it of its bishop's seat and gaining control of its trade, crafts and every other activity. In due course, the territory of Fiesole filled with villas built by the wealthy families of Florence and monasteries, soon becoming one of the most sought-after resorts for travellers in search of beauty and tranquillity, such as painters and writers, from Paul Klee to Marcel Proust. The town becomes very lively in the warmer months, when the festival of the "Estate Fiesolana" takes place. The ancient forum of the town has been replaced by **Piazza Mino da Fiesole**, with the 14th century **Praetorian Palace** at one end, flanked by the oratory of **Santa Maria Primerana**; the 11th century **Cathedral**, dedicated to St. Romulus runs along the length of the square. It underwent transformations in the 12th and 13th centuries and was heavily restored in the 19th century. The 13th century bell tower is the chief feature of the little town's skyline. The interior is austere, with a nave flanked by two side-aisles; some of the columns have Roman capitals. The raised presbitery possesses a main altar with a triptych by Bicci di Lorenzo. To the right of the altar is the Salutati Chapel, with frescoes by Cosimo Rosselli and statues by Mino da Fiesole. Next to the Cathedral is the **Bandini Museum**: della Robbia terracottas, paintings of the 12th-15th centuries the *Triumphs* of Jacopo del Sellaio and the *Madonna* by the Bigallo Master. The adjacent archaeological area is interesting, with a **Roman Theatre** first built towards the end of the 1st century A.D. and still in use during the warmer months for concerts and plays; the remains of a **Temple** and of the **Baths**; the **Archaeological Museum**: containing Etruscan and Roman finds, sculpture that used to be part of the theatre, Etruscan grave-stones with banquet scenes. From Piazza Mino da Fiesole one climbs up to the church and monastery of **St. Francis**. The site has been used by the Franciscan community since 1399 and was lived in for several years by St. Bernardino da Siena (whose tiny little cell can be seen in the diminutive monastery); the attraction of the place is, however, chiefly due to massive restoration, as only a few frescoes and the 16th century furnishings of the sacristy are original.

Beyond Fiesole one proceeds towards Borgunto, whereupon one turns right towards the **Castle of Vincigliata**, an ancient medieval keep which was in a state of disrepair until the middle of the last century, when it was bought by John Temple Leader who entrusted it to Giuseppe Fancelli to be restored. The

San Domenico - The marble façade of the Badia Fiesolana, an ancient church dominating the valley of the Mugnone; below: the interior.

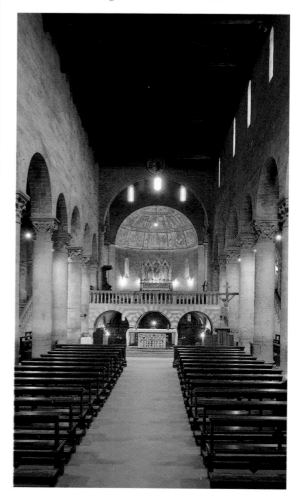

Fiesole - View of Piazza Mino, with the 13th century Cathedral bell tower; below: the church and monastery of San Francesco; right, from the top: the Roman Theatre and the remains of the Baths.

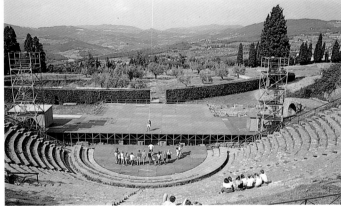

road winds along through cypress groves, such distinctive features of the Florentine landscape, until one reaches **Villa i Tatti**, which was bought in 1905 by the art-critic Bernard Berenson who had it restructured with the assistance of the architect Cecil Pinsent; villa, garden, library, sculpture collection and paintings were bequeathed by their owner to Harvard University.

Once one has reached Ponte a Mensola, one turns left into Via D'Annunzio and climbs up to Settignano, where Michelangelo's wet-nurse used to live.

Pratolino - The colossal Appennino statue, by Giambologna, in the park of Villa Demidoff.

SETTIGNANO

SETTIGNANO – An ancient medieval burg, which used to consist originally of a fairly sparse number of houses, famed in the past for having contained the workshops of numerous stone-masons.

The most famous stone-cutter became an artist of the first rank and was known as Desiderio da Settignano, a sculptor of the 15th century, whose statue stands triumphantly in the middle of the main square of the village. During the last century, Settignano became a residential centre and holiday resort of renown: Niccolò Tommaseo, Telemaco Signorini (the painter) and Gabriele D'Annunzio all lived there. The latter lived in **Villa la Capponcina** between 1898 and 1910, during which time one of his guests was Claude Debussy. The village contains the ancient church of **Santa Maria**, founded before the 12th century, but much restructured, chiefly in the 16th and 18th centuries; the *Madonna and Child*, in glazed terracotta, on the main altar, is by the workshop of Andrea della Robbia at the beginning of the 15th century, whilst the *Saint Lucy* above the second altar on the left is attributed to Michelozzo (1430). Of further interest in the village, see the **Oratory of the Holy Trinity**, the 19th century **Cemetery**, containing the tombs of Tommaseo and Aldo Palazzeschi, the **Oratory of St. Romano** and the **Oratory of Vannella** which contains a fresco attributed to Botticelli (c. 1470). A kilometre away from Settignano, in the direction of Compiobbi, is the **Villa Gamberaia**. Built as the unpretentious summer resort of a monastery, it was restructured by the Lapi and chiefly by the Capponi in the 17th and 18th centuries; the villa underwent further changes at the beginning of the 20th century, when it belonged to Princess Ghyka, sister to the Queen of Serbia. The Italianate garden, with its statues, beds, pools and flowering shrubs and its magnificent view of Florence down in the valley, is one of the best kept in Tuscany.

2. PRATOLINO, MONTESENARIO

From Ponte Rosso (in Florence) one takes the Via Bolognese and climbs up-hill flanked on either side by a succession of handsome buildings, mostly built in the 19th century, with – however – the occasional presence of more ancient patrician demesnes. Shortly after the first rise called the Pellegrino, one encounters the 18th century façade of **Santa Maria del Suffragio** which is of remarkable interest in view of the large number of original furnishings it contains. Further up, at La Pietra, is another magnificent example of 18th century architecture – **Villa La Pietra**, designed by Carlo Fontana, containing Sir Harold Acton's beautiful art collection and surrounded by a marvellously kept Italianate garden. After La Lastra, one passes Trespiano with the church of **Santa Lucia**, founded in the 13th century, but completely restructured in the 1930s. Shortly afterwards, a long wall on the right leads up to the entrance of the park of Villa Demidoff (or Medici Villa of Pratolino).

La Pietra - Villa La Pietra, designed by Carlo Fontana; below: a view of the gardens.

VILLA DEMIDOFF – The Villa has been re-opened to the public after long years of total neglect. It must have been one of the most beautiful among the many built by the Medici in the 16th century, if descriptions are anything to go by – a technological marvel rather than a master-piece of architectural design.

The Villa and the Park were designed between 1568 and 1581 by two of the most bizarre and inspired minds in Mannerist Forence: Prince Francesco Ist de' Medici – art lover and amateur alchemist rather than ruler and Bernardo Buontalenti, his friend and personal architect. The originality of their ideas can be briefly summarised as follows: the park is the main element of the complex and water is both "deus ex machina" and leading actor in the play. It flowed down from Montesenario forming pools, fountains, water-falls, setting dozens of automas in motion, it trickled into a series of grottoes making a miriad invisible birds break into song, it created tunnels of luminous jets of spray and set-off a whole series of surprising effects. Anyone lucky enough to visit the place during the first centuries of its existence was full of the wonders he or she experienced there. Francesco I's successors until Ferdinando de'Medici (end 17th century)) took care of Pratolino, even having a theatre built on the third

Settignano - Villa Gamberaia. Below: **La Pietra** - Another view of the splendid Italianate gardens of Villa La Pietra.

floor of the villa, to which musicians like Haendel and Alessandro Scarlatti were invited. Unfortunately the Hapsburg-Lorraine family decided that the up-keep of the whole complex was too expensive and transferred all the sculpture and other works of art to the town palaces and left the park and villa to look after themselves, which naturally led to their falling into complete disrepair. The central building was demolished in 1824 by the Bohemian architect Joseph Fritsch, who was asked to transform Pratolino into an English-style landscaped garden. The project was never completed. The next owners, the Demidoff family, used one of the subsidiary buildings as their residence. In 1969, the ancient furnishings were sold at auction. The spectacular complex that had caught the fancy of both Montaigne and De Sade (who set one of his tales there) is now an immense park which surrounds a few buildings such as the ex-villa of the Demidoffs and the cyclopic shape of the *Appennino*, the 19 metre high statue that Giambologna carved so that it would be mirrored in the lily-pool at its feet.

Beyond the villa one comes to the little village of **Pratolino**: via Bolognese proceeds towards the Mugello (see Itinerary 6 of the Province of Florence), whilst a road off right leads up to **Bivigliano**. The little village contains the small Romanesque church of **San Romolo**, where one can admire a glazed terracotta altar-piece by the Workshop of Andrea della Robbia (c. 1494). Beyond Bivigliano one climbs up to the **Monastery of Montesenario**. The monastery was founded on the 8th September 1233 by seven noble Florentines (the Seven Saints) who forsook the comforts of town life and withdrew to a hermitage where they founded the order of the Servants of Mary. After a disastrous earthquake in the 16th century, Montesenario experienced a period of remarkable splendour in the Baroque period, when the church and the monastery were filled with works of art.

3. Castello, Sesto Fiorentino

From the square of Careggi (that leads into the main Policlinic of Florence that includes and surrounds the ancient Medici Villa of Careggi, erstwhile splendid residence of the Magnificent Lorenzo), one takes Via Santo Stefano in Pane, thence right into Via delle Panche which leads into Via Giuliani; further on, to the right is via della Petraia leading up to the Medici Villa della Petraia.

VILLA DELLA PETRAIA – A magnificent complex, revealing the various periods (16th to 19th centuries) in which additions were made to it – it consists of a great villa that was used as a residence by the Medici and, during the last century by Victor Emanuel IInd) and an elegant Italianate garden leading up to a landscaped park in the English style, one of the few instances of the latter in the Florentine area.

In the 13th century, Petraia belonged to the Brunelleschi family, later it was owned by the Strozzi and then by the Medici family. Until the 15th century it preserved its fortified farm-house aspect, surrounded by stables, labourers' dwellings, an oven and even a small brick-oven and factory. Towards the middle of the 16th century Ferdinando de' Medici handed it over to Buontalenti with instructions to transform it into a seigneurial residence. The terraces and geometrically arranged parterre beds of the Italianate garden were laid out in the area in front of the façade of the building in the following century. The park behind the villa, that had been left "wild" up to that point, was landscaped in the English style by architect and landscape gardener Joseph Fritsch of Bohemia, who had already supplied a project for the Medici villa of Pratolino. When Florence was capital of Italy, the building became the private residence of Victor Emanuel IInd who changed most of the furnishings. The beautiful central courtyard (now covered by a glass roof) was frescoed by Volterrano between 1636 and 1648, illustrating the Glory of the Medici dynasty; see also the 17th century chapel, the splendid dining room and the private apartments of the King (interesting party games).

Leaving Petraia one turns back a short while and takes the road to the right that leads one to the ex-Royal Villa of Castello.

VILLA DI CASTELLO – Magnificent example of 16th century architecture. The villa is Cosimo I's and his architect Tribolo's masterpiece. The latter designed the lovely Italianate garden (on the side of the park nearest the house, behind the villa) which was to be copied and reproduced throughout Europe.

The first Medici to own the villa were Lorenzo and Giovanni di Pierfrancesco who bought it in 1477. Grand Duke Cosimo I commissioned Tribolo to lay out a

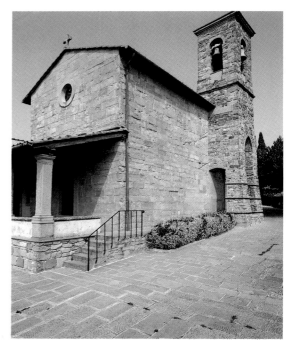

Bivigliano - The parish church of San Romolo.

Montesenario - The square in front of the Monastery.

Castello - The statue of January, by Bartolommeo Ammannati, in the park of the Medici villa.

Sesto Fiorentino - Villa La Petraia, an ancient Medieval castle, restructured by Bernardo Buontalenti for Ferdinando I de' Medici. Below: **Castello** - The elegant façade of the Medici villa, now the headquarters of the Accademia della Crusca.

garden behind the villa in 1541 giving him very precise and detailed instructions as to the allegorical allusions to the glorious quality of Cosimo's rulership that were to be woven into the garden's design. The parterre garden not only included the *Hercules and Cacus* fountain but also the famous *Venus*, by Giambologna; the delightful *Animal Grotto* opens onto the parterre garden from its end wall; on the upper level, the statue of *January* by Ammannati is reflected in the pond surrounding it; all around a "wild" boschetto or grove, of oaks and ilexes. The main building, which was continually resided in by the grand ducal family, used to contain the *Dance of Spring* and the *Birth of Venus* by Botticelli, in Cosimo's lifetime. The Hapsburgh- Lorraine and Savoy families both used it as their residence too. Today it houses the Accademia della Crusca, the prestigious institute of linguistic studies founded in 1583.

Once back on via Giuliani, one proceeds towards Sesto. (The road becomes Via Gramsci). Via Gaddi, on the right, leads up to **Quinto**, where there are a number of interesting patrician mansions and Etruscan tombs, the most remarkable of which is the **Montagnola**, a large 7th century B.C. tumulus.

SESTO FIORENTINO – Once a prevalently agricultural market-town, surrounded by farms and large estates, it is situated six Roman miles from Florence and underwent a complete transformation of its economic and social prospects in the 18th century, when Marquis Ginori founded the Doccia porcelain factory. The production of majolica and porcelain absorbed most of the labour force in the area and endowed the town with a certain amount of renown even beyond the confines of Tuscany.

Although most of the town buildings are modern, some interesting traces of the past emerge here and there. **Villa Corsi-Salviati**, built in the 15th and 16th centuries possesses a magnificent garden laid out in the 17th and 18th centuries. In the centre of the town we find the **Praetorian Palace** and the Romanesque **Parish of San Martino**; beyond the town of Sesto, in the direction of Prato, one encounters the **museum of Doccia porcelain**, housing examples from the most significant types of porcelain produced over three hundred years by one of the most famous and ancient factories in Europe.

Sesto Fiorentino - One of the rooms in the Museum of Porcelain of Doccia; below: soup-tureen of the II half of the 18th century, Ginori Collection.

4. CERTOSA DEL GALLUZZO

From Porta Romana one takes the Via Senese, which follows the old Via Cassia, the road that used to lead from Florence to Rome. After the rise of San Gaggio, one arrives in the village of Galluzzo. Shortly after the village, one descries to the right, on the top of the hill of Monteacuto, the superbly elegant forms of the Certosa or Chartreuse.

CERTOSA DEL GALLUZZO – Together with the Chartreuse of Pavia, it is one of the most beautiful in Italy. Founded towards the middle of the 14th century, it has managed to preserve most of its original lines, notwithstanding the many successive alterations. It is deservedly famous, both because of the serene harmony of the structure with the surrounding hilly scenery, as well as for its truly remarkable cycle of frescoes by Pontormo.

The monastic complex was founded in 1342 by Niccolò Acciaioli, who descended from an ancient Florentine family and became Grand Seneschal to the King of Naples in the Angevin period. The distance that separated the monastery from the town led the builders to strengthen its fortifications. One of the most distinctive aspects of the Carthusian Order (a traditional outlet for the younger sons and daughters of most of the Italian nobility), other than the severity of its rule was its close relationship with the world of culture; which explains the superb library and well-endowed painting collection in the monastery. The halls of the picture gallery also contain the detached frescoed lunettes illustrating *Episodes from the Life of Jesus*, by Pontormo painted in the 1520s. See also works by Ridolfo del Ghirlandaio, Raffaellino del Garbo, Rutilio Manetti and l'Empoli. The heart of the monastery, which is a veritable fortified citadel, is the church of **San Lorenzo**, which was restructured towards the middle of the 16th century. The interior is divided into two sections, with the part reserved to the monks (where the 14th century structure is still in evidence) separated from the rest of the church; the choir stalls carved and inlaid are magnificent in both sections; from the chapel of Santa Maria one descends to a series of underground chapels in which one finds the tombs of the Acciaioli family: the *tomb of Nicolò Acciaioli* is of particular interest and is attributed to Orcagna's workshop (c. 1365).

CHARTREUSE OF GALLUZZO - Crucifixion, by Mariotto Albertinelli.

Galluzzo - The austere Chartreuse, in admirable harmony with the surrounding softly rolling landscape; below: the fine cloisters.

THE PROVINCE OF FLORENCE

Carmignano - The parish church of San Michele; below: the cloister.

1. Poggio a Caiano, Artimino — 2. Prato — 3. Empoli, Vinci, Cerreto Guidi — 4. Valdelsa and Certaldo — 5. The Chianti from Impruneta to Greve — 6. The Mugello.

1. POGGIO A CAIANO, ARTIMINO

This itinerary winds through the area to the north-west of Florence around the Via Pistoiese. The main points of interest are a number of Etruscan tombs and above all the two Medici villas of Poggio a Caiano and Artimino. The latter, together with the Villas of Quarrata and Cerreto Guidi (see also Itinerary 3 of the Province of Florence) constituted a kind of defensive-residential square surrounding an immense hunting-ground (the enclosing wall of which is still partially extant) which virtually included the whole Montalbano terrain. The centre of **Poggio a Caiano** rises on the first hillocks of Montalbano and the villa is situated at the top of the highest rise.

The **MEDICI VILLA OF POGGIO A CAIANO** – It is perhaps the most beautiful amongst Lorenzo the Magnificent's villas. He bought it in 1480 and handed it over to Giuliano da Sangallo to be restructured. The villa was sung by Poliziano in his poem *L'Ambra*; over the following centuries it witnessed the mysterious deaths of Francesco I and Bianca Cappello (1587), the manic ravings of Marguerite Louise d'Orléans, wife to Cosimo III, and romantic encounters of Victor Emanuel II with the Duchess of Mirafiori. Since 1919 it has belonged to the Italian State.

An extensive garden surrounds the house, leading out on the rear into a great park. The elegant central edifice surrounded on all sides by an airy portico possesses a classical, loggia-shaped, 16th century main entrance with a blue and white enamelled frieze, the design of which is attributed to Sansovino. On the ground floor are the apartments of Bianca Cappello. On the first floor, which was partially restructured for Victor Emanuel IInd is the magnificent ball-room (which is so high-ceilinged that it takes up the second floor as well) with its walls covered by the *frescoes* considered among the greatest ever painted by the Mannerist School: the themes are centred on Roman history and mythology: the better known artists responsible for the frescoes include Alessandro Allori, Andrea del Sarto and Pontormo (who painted the scene with *Vertumnus* and *Pomona* – 1521 – in the lunette above the right wall). The dining room and the apartments of the king of Italy are also of interest.

Artimino - The parish church of San Leonardo.

Leaving Poggio a Caiano in the direction of Pistoia, one turns left towards **Carmignano**. The old burg's parish church of **San Michele** possesses a magnificent *Visitation* by Pontormo. A road off to the left leads to **Artimino**. A tranquil, silent little village with most of its fortifications intact together with its ancient castle and its picturesque walls. It is famed for the wine produced on the slopes all around the village. The parish church of **San Leonardo**, founded in 1107 by the Countess Matilda, contains wooden sculpture of the 14th and 15th century, a Della Robbia glazed terracotta relief and bears a Roman carved relief set into the façade of the church which gives one some idea of the ancient origins of the building. The Medici Villa is situated at the top of the hill opposite the village of Artimino.

LA FERDINANDA – Built for Ferdinando Ist de' Medici to designs by Bernardo Buontalenti, at the end of the 16th century – it presents a curious appearance, due to the enormous number of chimneys studded all over its roof and is the Medici villa that was most affected by its hunting-lodge function.

Every ornamental accessory has been reduced to the minimum with the sole exception of the elegantly designed stairway and loggia of access: no garden, which would have revealed that the building was also intended to be used as a residence; its park is the forest, the vast hunting reserve of Montalbano. Even the numerous chimneys owe their presence to hunting requirements: each one leads down to a fireplace in one of the many rooms in the villa, which had to be heated during the winter months, the months traditionally devoted to hunting expeditions by the Medici family. The underground part of the villa has been transformed into an attractive museum, filled with Etruscan and Roman finds

Poggio a Caiano - The Medici Villa restructured by Giuliano da Sangallo for Lorenzo de' Medici, the Magnificent; below: the side of the villa seen from the garden. **Artimino** - The Medici Villa known as «Ferdinanda», designed by Buontalenti for Ferdinando I.

dug-up in the area surrounding Artimino, that has proved particularly generous from an archaeological point of view.

There are a number of Etruscan necropoli in the vicinity of Artimino. An Etruscan town used to be situated on the ridge between the villa and the village between the 7th and 2nd century B.C. A number of tumulus tombs containing utensils and weapons as well as gold-smiths' artifacts revealing contacts with the craftsmen of Volterra and Fiesole. The finds discovered around **Comeana** (off the road linking Artimino to Carmignano) are of particular interest; there is a pseudo-cupola-type tomb near Montefortini which has been dated around the 7th century B.C.

2. PRATO

PRATO – An industrial town, one of the most important centres for the production of woollen fabrics, with a medieval nucleus, of great artistic interest, surrounded by its 14th century six-sided fortifications.

Originally, there seems to have been an Etrusco-Roman settlement which rose in a favourable position, not far from the Via Cassia, which developed gradually (it seems to have been known as Pagus Cornius as from the 9th century). Starting from the 12th century its craftsmen and merchants appear to have flourished and expanded choosing to range their Free Commune first on the side of the Ghibellines, then on the Guelph side. The town continued to prosper even after Florence conquered it in 1351. At the heart of the medieval nucleus is the **Cathedral Square** with the 12th century Romanesque **Cathedral of Santo Stefano** (it was founded in the 10th century but was restructured and enlarged over the centuries), the façade, in alternating bands of white and green marble was finished in the 15th century. The *Pulpit of the Holy Girdle*, a masterpiece by Donatello (1438) supported by a bronze capital by Michelozzo is on the right outer corner of the façade: the original reliefs by the Florentine master (*Dance of cherubs*) are to be seen in the nearby **Museo dell'Opera del Duomo**. A glazed terracotta *Madonna and Child*, by Andrea della Robbia (1489) is in the lunette above the main entrance. The Romanesque-Gothic belltower (12th-14th centuries) with twin and triple mullioned arched windows soars up to the right of the church. Inside, the nave is divided from the side-aisles by spinach-green marble columns; immediately to the left, a 15th century grille encloses the 14th century Chapel of the Holy Girdle, frescoed by Agnolo Gaddi with a *Madonna and Child* sculpted by Giovanni Pisano. The Chapel shelters the Holy Girdle, a precious relique of the Virgin, donated to the cathedral by a rich and adventurous merchant of Prato, one Michele Dagomari; the most interesting items in the cathedral, however, are two frescoed cycles: one on the apse, depicting *Episodes from the Lives of St. John the Baptist and St. Stephen*, by Filippo Lippi (one of the greatest Florentine masters of the 15th century and teacher to Botticelli), which can be considered one of the most remarkable examples of Renaissance painting; the other, also of great note, is in the chapel to the right of the presbitery and is attributed to Paolo Uccello. A few steps away from the Cathedral is the little square of the Commune, where one finds the **Praetorian Palace** (Palazzo Pretorio), built in the 13th and 14th centuries, with an external stairway and balcony (the oldest part is in brick); it houses an interesting **Gallery** that contains works by Florentine masters of the 14th and 15th centuries as well as a collection of plaster-casts collected by the famous nineteenth century sculptor and native of Prato, Lorenzo Bartolini. The neighbouring Piazza delle Carceri is dominated by the gleaming white **Emperor's Castle** (Castello dell'Imperatore), a square-walled and battlemented structure (the battlements are Ghibelline); the only one of its kind in Central-Northern Italy and in perfect condition, it was built towards the first half of the 13th century, by order of Frederick IInd; its appearance is identical to the many Swabian fortresses built at that time in the South of Italy. A variety of cultural events are staged nowadays in the inner courtyard. Nearby, one encounters the church of **Santa Maria delle Carceri** (1484-1495), a masterpiece by Giuliano da Sangallo and one of the greatest examples of Renaissance architecture: a Greek cross structure with a dome above the crossing, the decoration and organisation of the space is strikingly stark, off-setting a remarkable series of glazed terracotta reliefs by Andrea della Robbia. Other churches of note include those of **San Francesco** and **San Domenico**. Prato's cultural liveliness and awareness of the latest developments and aspects of art have led to the creation of the very innovative **Museum of Contemporary Art** built outside the town's central area. Not far from the medieval nucleus of the town, one comes to Piazza San Marco, where a statue by the famous contemporary sculptor, Henry Moore has been placed.

Prato - Piazza del Comune.

Prato - Santa Maria delle Carceri; below: the Museum of Contemporary Art, founded recently in the outskirts of the town.

Prato - Cathedral of Santo Stefano with the pulpit of the Holy Girdle, by Donatello; below: the towering white Castle of the Emperor.

This itinerary leads one along the initial stretches of the lower Valdarno, towards Pisa. After Ponte a Signa, the Arno river runs through the narrow, picturesque gully of the Gonfolina.

EMPOLI – The town has grown to its present size on the left bank of the river Arno, at the meeting point of important trade routes and was, and still is, an important trading and agricultural centre (*Emporium*).

The original Roman settlement, which was almost certainly a river port, used to be situated in the area that is still known as Empoli Vecchio (Old Empoli). During the Middle Ages, the town expanded eastwards and the core of modern Empoli is centered around the Parish Church of Sant'Andrea. Its first feudal lords were the counts Guidi, then it became part of the territory of Florence. After the Guelph party was defeated at Montaperti (1260), Empoli became the headquarters of the famous "Ghibelline Parliament" which was supposed to decide how Tuscany was to be partitioned and governed and what the fate of Florence was to be; the latter was luckily saved from destruction by the generous intervention of Farinata degli Uberti. In 1530. The heart of the town is Piazza Farinata degli Uberti, where one encounters the **Ghibelline Palace**, which was restructured in the 16th century, and was formerly the headquarters of the famous "Parliament", as well as the **Collegiata di Sant'Andrea** (Parish Church of St. Andrew), which was restructured in 1093 in Florentine Romanesque style, – further restructuring took place in the 18th century. The original white and green marble façade with its five arches is still visible on the lower level, whereas the upper portion was added in the 18th century. The **Museo della Collegiata**, that contains valuable works by Tuscan masters of the 14th to the 17th centuries, including veritable masterpieces, such as the *Deposition*, by Masolino da Panicale, is to the right of the church.

In Empoli, one leaves the main Pisan road and climbs gradually up to Montalbano and San Baronto, until one reaches Vinci.

VINCI – The little village is surrounded by the thick vegetation of the Montalbano hills, where one is struck by the changing greens of the olive groves and vineyards. The village grew up around the castle of the Counts Guidi and was conquered by Florence in the 13th century. It owes its fame to Leonardo who was born here on the 15th April 1452.

One can start visiting the village in the **Vinci Museum**, which is arranged on two of the floors of the old castle. The collection includes a large number of models, reproduced to scale in recent times and based on Leonardo's drawings, which are arranged in facsimile next to each of the models of the machines designed by the brilliant artist and scientist. The same building also houses the **Leonardo Library** which promotes a whole series of cultural activities aimed at promoting the study of Leonardo's complex works and celebrating his memory (including Vinci Readings and an aerial event). Whether one is roaming within the realms of fact or legend, it is pleasant to walk up to the **Parish Church of Santa Croce**, where one can admire the baptismal font supposedly used at the christening of Leonardo; a few kilometres outside the village, in the spot known as **Anchiano**, where one can see the old farm house (that was restored in 1952) believed to be where the artist first entered this world on that remote 15th April (the guardian will show one around).

Leaving Vinci one returns down towards the Arno river until one reaches Cerreto Guidi.

CERRETO GUIDI – It rises upon a hill that used formerly to be covered by Turkey oaks (Cerro – whence Cerreto). The village was called Cerreto di Greti until it became a feudal holding of the Counts Guidi, in the 11th century. The Guidi family were very powerful all over the area but had to renounce their claim on Cerreto Guidi in the 12th century when they sold their rights to the Commune of Florence.

In 1576 it witnessed a bloody act of murder which took place in the main attraction of the place -- the Medici villa overlooking the village. The actors in the tragedy were Paolo Giordano Orsini, duke of Bracciano and his spouse, Isabella de' Medici, daughter to Cosimo I de' Medici. The former being the murderer, the latter the victim. It was the old, old story of the husband wreaking his hurt pride on his faithless consort. Thus poor lonely Isabella fell in love with her husband's cousin, Troilus Orsini, who paid her more attention than her ever-absent husband, and was thereupon strangled by a diabolical contrivance, in her bed. Like other Medici Villas, the **Medici Villa of Cerreto**

Empoli - The cloister of the Collegiata (Sant'Andrea); below: the entrance to the Museum of the Collegiata, off Piazzetta San Giovanni.

Vinci - The Castle of the Counts Guidi, the headquarters of the Vinci Museum and of the Leonardian Library.

Empoli - The church of Santa Maria a Ripa. Below, right: **Vinci** - A room in the Vinci Museum.

Vinci - Above and below: two more views of the Vinci Museum rooms.

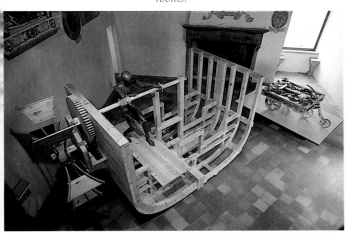

Guidi was first built as a summer resort and hunting lodge. It was commissioned in the 16th century by Cosimo I and the original project was probably by Bernardo Buontalenti. The main body of the villa, which enjoys a magnificent view over the Valdinievole, consists of a compact block supporting the massive structure of the access ramps, designed by Buontalenti between 1565 and 1567.

4. VALDELSA AND CERTALDO

The itinerary can be considered a sort of extension of the preceding one. After leaving Empoli, one proceeds towards Pisa until one reaches **Ponte a Elsa**. Leaving Ponte a Elsa one bears south along the State road No. 429 which traverses the Valdelsa, revealing a prevalently hilly landscape, distinguished by numerous vineyards. **Castelfiorentino** crowns a hilltop that dominates the valley. The village contains the Baroque, 18th century church of **Santa Verdiana**: the saint to whom the church is dedicated is supposed to have stayed walled up in a cell (which one can visit in the church crypt) together with a pair of serpents, for 34 years. There is a fascinating **Collection of Paintings** in the rectory next door, that includes a polyptych by Taddeo Gaddi, works by the Schools of Ghirlandaio, Filippino Lippi, and Andrea del Sarto as well as illuminated choral manuscript books. From Castelfiorentino, a side-road leads off towards **Montaione**, an old, fortified, medieval burg, as well as to the **Monastery of San Vivaldo**, which is a Franciscan hermitage buried deep in the heart of a thick forest, with a central body and a series of 16th century chapels scattered through the wood (like the "holy mounts") each one of which contains terracotta groups depicting episodes from the life of Christ. The monastery was founded on the site in memory of a hermit from San Gimignano named Vivaldo who was found dead inside a hollow chestnut tree, which he had withdrawn to, to spend the rest of his life in prayer (1322).

From Montaione, one can return to the Valdelsa state road via **Gambassi**, an ancient hot springs site, reaching Certaldo.

CERTALDO – An agricultural-industrial centre with a fortified medieval nucleus at the top of a hill (the **Castle**) which is particularly picturesque because of the brick used throughout the whole old town, both on the private dwellings (many of which were restructured in the 15th century, in accordance with the building techniques adopted in the Middle Ages), as well as for the paving of the streets. Giovanni Boccaccio, whose father was a native of Certaldo, spent the latter years of his life here, until his death in 1375.

Tradition has placed the residence of the great man of letters in the dwelling known as **Boccaccio's House**, a building that has been completely restructured fairly recently, replacing a preexistent construction (which was possibly itself rebuilt on the site of even earlier house) dating from the 15th century. At present the National Centre of Studies on Boccaccio has its headquarters here, as well as a library housing a wide selection of volumes on Boccaccio's writings and numerous editions of his work. If one climbs up to the loggia and tower, one enjoys a beautiful view. Not far off is the church of **Saints Michael and James**, of the 13th century, which has been restored several times during this century: it possesses a lovely 14th century cloister, to the left of the church; the two Della Robbia shrines on either side of the main altar, inside, are worthy of note, see also the Cenotaph dedicated to Boccaccio (on the right wall) together with a bust of the poet sculpted in 1503 by Giovanni Francesco Rustici. A little further on, one encounters the **Praetorian Palace** or Vicar's Quarters. It belonged to the Counts Alberti until the 13th century, thereafter it became the residence of the Podestà or of the Florentine Delegate (Vicar): it was restored at the end of the last century, after an earlier restructuring between the 15th and 16th centuries; a number of fragments of frescoes by Benozzo Gozzoli and Giusto d'Andrea have been arranged inside the *Chapel of St. Thomas*, which opens off the charming courtyard.

5. THE CHIANTI, FROM IMPRUNETA TO GREVE

This itinerary winds through an extensive part of the area between Florence and Siena, which is prevalently hilly and of remarkable interest, both because of its landscape and artistic assets (see also the itinerary for the province of Siena). The Chianti is the land of wine, vineyards, great farmsteads and castles. Notwithstanding the extensive vineyards, (which lend a man-modelled aspect to the landscape) there are also considerably widespread wooded areas (beech,

Monastery of San Vivaldo - 16th century chapels.

Certaldo - View; below: the Praetorian Palace.

Castelfiorentino - The Baroque façade of Santa Verdiana. Below: **Certaldo** - The birthplace of Giovanni Boccaccio and a lovely view of the Chianti countryside.

chestnut, as well as Mediterranean scrub and umbrella-pine woods (near Strada in Chianti). The most constant and familiar presence, however, marking boundaries, paths, casting its tall shadow over a farm house or tracing the contours of a hilltop is the cypress. One can start from Galluzzo (see itinerary 4 for the surroundings of Florence), where one takes the Via Cassia, proceeding towards **Tavarnuzze** (interesting church of **San Lorenzo** and **Villa Antinori**), then one goes on to Bagnolo and Impruneta.

IMPRUNETA

IMPRUNETA – A large town, drawing its livelihood from a variety of economic resources: agricultural, production of terracotta, brick and tiles, and wine, as well as tourism (as it has become a pleasant holiday resort), it is of considerable interest from various points of view.

In the 11th century it became an important centre due to the presence of a sanctuary dedicated to the veneration of an image of a Madonna and Child, which legend reports was painted by St. Luke the Evangelist and first brought by Romulus, a disciple of St. Peter, to Fiesole (his Bishopric), whence it was removed to safety by a number of early Christians who had managed to escape the Roman persecutions, and hidden at the top of a hill in the middle of a bramble spinney ("in pruinetis" = amidst the brambles), whence the name of Impruneta. The town later became part of the territory of Florence and it earned much renown thanks to the important Fair of St. Luke which attracted immense crowds and was depicted chiefly by 16th and 17th century painters. The most important building is the basilica of **Santa Maria dell'Impruneta**, founded in the 11th century and much restructured, specially in the 15th century. The bell tower is of the 13th century, whereas the portico across the façade is of the 17th century. Inside, one is immediately struck by the beauty of the two presbitery shrines, by Michelozzo (1453-1456): both of them decorated with lovely Della Robbia glazed terracotta reliefs; the one on the left contains the much venerated, ancient and Byzantine-looking icon of the *Madonna and Child*, the basilica was first built to shelter. The polyptych on the main altar, as well as being a Florentine 14th century masterpiece, is a miracle of modern restoration technique, as it was shattered into 2000 pieces by a IInd World War bomb. There is another 14th century polyptych in the baptistery; the sacristy and the delightful cloisters are also worth a visit.

From Impruneta, one proceeds towards **Strada in Chianti**, thence southwards along the Chiantigiana state highway until Greve.

GREVE

GREVE – It is situated on the banks of the river Greve, in the heart of the Rooster Chianti area, which produces a prestigious wine that is the focal point of the annual September Market Show.

Its position on the Chiantigiana way is recalled in the Middle Ages when it is mentioned as the market town used by the nearby castle and estate of Montefioralle as their trading post. Greve's subservient status as regards the feudal lords of Montefioralle, came to an end when the fortunes of the latter started to decline towards the 16th century, allowing Greve to develop and grow independently. The main square — **Piazza del Mercatale** — nowadays called piazza Matteotti, has an unusual asymmetrical, roughly triangular shape, with porticoes topped by terraces running all the way around. At the end of the square is the church of *Santa Croce*, which was totally reconstructed in the 19th century; inside the church one can admire a 15th century triptych by Bicci di Lorenzo (*Annunciation*) as well as a painting by the so-called Master of Greve of the 13th century (*Madonna and Saints*). Not far away, inside the **Oratory of San Francesco**, one finds an interesting 16th century glazed terracotta group of the *Deposition with the three Maries and three Saints*. Two kilometres from Greve, at the top of a hill is the picturesque village of **Montefioralle** where the ruins of the castle walls still survive and the old towers have been transformed into charming dwellings; see also the Medieval church of **Santo Stefano** and the house traditionally held to be the birth place of Amerigo Vespucci.

6. THE MUGELLO

This route runs along a wide semicircular valley for about 30 kilometres, to the north of Florence, flanked by two parallel lines of hills separated by the bed of the river Sieve that is fed by a host of streams and rivulets. Inhabited since time immemorial (traces of Neolithic, and later settlements have been found all over the area); in the Middle Ages, it became one of the favourite places for the Florentines to build their summer resorts in. The Medici family were natives of the Mugello, imbibing its farming and mercantile traditions. The region is still basilically untouched by the great communication routes (the Autostrada del

Montefioralle - View; below: the birthplace of Amerigo Vespucci.

Impruneta - The Basilica of Santa Maria dell'Impruneta. Below: **Greve** - The monument to Giovanni da Verrazzano in Piazza del Mercatale, renamed Matteotti and view of the square itself.

Sole has an exit at Barberino) which has enabled the traditional life-styles to survive both in the countryside and in the towns.

The road traversing all the main centres in the Mugello starts in **Barberino di Mugello** and follows the course of the Sieve river until it flows into the Arno at Pontassieve. On ones way down to San Piero a Sieve, one encounters a road leading-off left towards the *Monastery of Bosco ai Frati*. The ancient Franciscan monastery was reconstructed, by order of Cosimo the Elder, by Michelozzo between 1420 and 1438; it used to possess three fine crucifixes — one small terracotta one by the Della Robbia school, another attributed to Desiderio da Settignano and one by Donatello (some critics attribute it, interestingly enough, to Michelozzo). In **Cafaggiolo** there is a beautiful **Medici Villa**, an erstwhile fortress, restructured by Michelozzo. Another fortress, called **San Martino**, designed in 1571 by Bernardo Buontalenti crowns the hill above **San Piero a Sieve**, whereas one encounters Michelozzo's handwork once again at the **Castle of Trebbio**. From San Piero a road climbs up to the Giogo pass traversing **Scarperia**, an ancient little town founded by the Florentines as a garrison post and famed for its production of steel blades and knives. The imposing **Praetorian Palace**, with its battlements and armorial bearings, overlooks the main square. Nearby one finds the **Oratory of the Madonna di Piazza**, where one can admire works by Jacopo del Casentino. Works by Matteo Rosselli, a *Crucifix* attributed to Sansovino, a *Madonna* by Benedetto da Maiano and a shrine by Mino da Fiesole are in the **Prepositurale** (church). In the neighbouring hamlet of **Sant'Agata**, there is a magnificent Romanesque **Parish Church**. One can, on the other hand, proceed along the Sieve until one reaches Borgo San Lorenzo.

Monastery of Bosco ai Frati - The church of the monastery.

BORGO SAN LORENZO

BORGO SAN LORENZO – A Florentine possession since the 14th century, it is the capital of the Mugello area (capoluogo). It is an important agricultural market town and boasts a number of fairly large industrial plants.

In 1919, an earthquake seriously damaged the whole town, doing grave injury to its artistic treasures, specially to the buildings. The church of **San Lorenzo**, founded in the 12th century, but owing most of its appearance to the 16th century, contains some interesting works by Matteo Rosselli and by the Circle of Perugino (*St. Sebastian between Saints Macarius and Vincent*), an 18th century domed central-plan building worthy of note. Not far from the centre of the town, along the road leading towards Faenza, one meets the beautiful Romanesque Parish Church of *San Giovanni Maggiore*: see the 11th century bell tower, which has an octagonal upper portion, and a marble inlaid pulpit inside the church.

One resumes the road leading along the Sieve valley and reaches the fork that leads one off left towards **Vespignano**, a minute rural hamlet which had the privilege of being Giotto's birthplace. The house, in which tradition reports he was born, can be visited and contains a little museum. Another great painter was born in neighbouring **Vicchio**: the Dominican Friar Angelico. Vicchio is another of the valley settlements that was fortified by Florence in 1295. At the end of the valley, where the hills close to form a sort of gully, one reaches Dicomano, at the crossing of the road that, via the Muraglione pass, leads up to Forlì.

Sant'Agata - The lovely Romanesque parish church.

Vicchio - Monument to Giotto in the middle of the square named after him.

DICOMANO

DICOMANO – An ancient Etrusco-Roman settlement, it was an important agricultural and manufacturing centre where a wide variety of crafts have been practiced for centuries.

The most important building in the town is the church of **Santa Maria**, founded in the 12th century, in the severest Romanesque style (partially restructured in the 16th century); above the second altar on the right is a *Marriage of St. Anne and St. Joachim* in terracotta, by the Della Robbia Circle. See also a *Madonna of the Carmel*, attributed to Vasari as well as a *Nativity*, by Bronzino's Circle. Not far off, is the **Chapel of the Santissima Annunziata** with a fresco by a Master of Piero della Francesca's Circle. From Dicomano one takes the state road Nr. 67 up to **San Godenzo**, which is a charming holiday resort and possesses a magnificent **Abbey**. The Benedictine monastery was built in the 11th century and possesses a 14th century *polyptych* by a Master of the School of Giotto, a wooden *St. Sebastian* by Baccio d'Agnolo (1507) and, in the crypt, the remains of St. Gaudentius, a friar of the 6th century.

Beyond Dicomano one proceeds along the Sieve and passes through the wine producing town of **Rufina**, arriving at length in **Pontassieve**, which is still important chiefly because of its wine production and its modern architecture. Nearby, however, one can visit the **Monastery of Santa Maria di Rosano**, founded in the 7th century and restructured in the 12th century.

Cafaggiolo - The beautiful Medici Villa restructured by Michelozzo.

San Piero a Sieve - The fortress of San Martino, 16th century.
Rufina - View.

Scarperia - Overall view.
Pontassieve - The Medici bridge over the Sieve.

PISTOIA

One of the many nursery gardens in the Pistoia area.

Little remains of the Roman town of *Pistoia*, where Catiline's rebellion against Rome was put down in 62 B.C. Its period of glory was the communal age (12th-14th century) when it rivalled Lucca and Florence as a trade center. In 1530 it fell to Florence, a blow from which it never recovered. Today it is a pleasant town, renowned for its nurseries and the nearby winter resort of *Abetone*.

RECOMMENDED ITINERARY – Start your tour in *Piazza del Duomo*, around which stand most of the city's major historical monuments: the **Duomo**, the *Baptistry, Palazzo del Comune, Palazzo del Vescovado*, and *Palazzo Pretorio* (covered with emblems and dated 1367). The square constitutes one of the most remarkable complexes of medieval architecture in existence. Take the narrow street between the Cathedral and Palazzo del Comune which intersects with Via Pacini and descend to **San Bartolomeo in Pantano**. Then retrace your steps to Via Pacini and turn right to reach the **Ospedale del Ceppo**. Proceed, making a left into Via delle Pappe, Via del Carmine, and then go right on Via Sant'Andrea, along which you find the church of **Sant'Andrea**. Continue along Via Sant'Andrea to the 14th century church of *San Francesco* on *Piazza Mazzini*. Take Via Bozzi and Via Curtatone e Montanara in the direction of midtown to Via della Madonna and the church of **Madonna dell'Umiltà**. Continue down Via Buozzi to *Piazza Gavinana*. Then, beyond **San Giovanni Fuorcivitas**, turn left into Via Cavour. In the outskirts (on the road to Montecatini) is Pistoia's renowned **Zoo**.

DUOMO – The 12th-13th century building has a typically Pisan Romanesque facade adorned with arcading and loggias. Della Robbia terracottas adorn the portal lunette and a section of the portico ceiling. Alongside is 13th century belltower.

The single-aisle interior features a typical Romanesque plan (e.g., raised choir-lowered crypt). It is filled with notable works of art, including the 14th century *Tomb of Cino da Pistoia* (right aisle), a lovely century bronze *candlestick* (choir), a *Virgin and Child* by Lorenzo di Credi (left choir aisle), and, in the *Cappella di San Jacopo* off the right aisle, a stupendous *silver altar frontal* with reliefs *depicting Biblical stories* and *scenes from the life of St. Jacob*, to which several masters contributed between the 13th and 15th centuries. In addition there are Romanesque sculptures in the *crypt* and an interesting collection of sculpture and painting, miniatures, and reliquaries in the **Museo Capitolare** (reached by way of the sacristy).

BAPTISTRY – This elegant Gothic building was designed by Andrea Pisano in the 14th century with a striking patterned facing.

PALAZZO DEL COMUNE – This delightful gothic building dates from the late 12th-13th centuries. The facade with its pointed-arch portico and Gothic windows is particularly striking. The interior (which still bears part of its original decoration) is Pistoia's city hall and a museum (**Museo Civico**, third floor). The collection focuses on Tuscan art, from the school of Berlinghieri, Daddi, Lorenzo di Credi, Ghirlandaio, up through 19th century masters.

SAN BARTOLOMEO IN PANTANO – The lintel on the central portal of this attractive Romanesque church (founded in 1159) bears a notable relief depicting *Christ teaching to the Apostles* attributed to Gruamonte. The plain interior vaunts fine carved capitals, 14th century frescoes (fragments), and a 14th century wooden *Crucifix*, but the real highlight is the great Romanesque *pulpit* on lion and telamon columns dominating the nave, which was carved in 1250 by Guido da Como. The subjects of the reliefs around the pulpit are *scenes from the life of Christ*, while *statues of saints* and *evangelist symbols* adorn the rest.

OSPEDALE DEL CEPPO – The hospital (founded around the turn of the 13th century) was named for the rough-hewn alms bowls (*ceppo*,

The Communal Palace, housing the Civic Museum; below: the fine Romanesque church of San Bartolommeo in Pantano.

The Cathedral and the Bell Tower; below: the Baptistery and the Praetorian Palace.

literally small treetrunk). Over the 16th century portico runs a glazed terracotta *frieze* of striking effect. The famous reliefs, executed by the della Robbia workshop in the 1500s, depict *Seven Charitable Deeds* with *Virtues* inbetween each one and in the tondos above the columns.

SANT'ANDREA – The reliefs of the architrave on the central portal of the 12th century church of Sant'Andrea were carved by Gruamonte and Adeodato in 1166. Their subjects are the *Wise Men before Herod* and the *Adoration of the Magi*. The highlight of the interior (aside from a Pisan school *baptismal font* and a wooden *Crucifix* by Giovanni Pisano) is the hexagonal *pulpit* on seven columns, with lions and human figures, also by Giovanni Pisano, on the left side. Ranked as one of the greatest masterpieces of Gothic sculpture, the carved pulpit, (c. 1300) is decorated with *scenes from the life of Christ* in the Pisan Gothic style that reached its acme in Giovanni.

MADONNA DELL'UMILTÀ – The architect of this early 16th century church, Ventura Vitoni, was clearly inspired by Brunelleschi's Renaissance designs. The elegant interior consists of a vestibule and a vast rectangular hall. The dome was designed by Vasari in 1561.

SAN GIOVANNI FUORCIVITAS – This 12th-13th century church lacks a finished facade (whereas the visible side is faced with patterned marbles). The portal architrave is adorned with a relief of the *Last Supper* carved by Gruamonte in 1162. Inside are several notable works, including a Pisan-style *holy water font*, a *pulpit* with *New Testament scenes* carved by Guglielmo da Pisa (1270), an *altarpiece* by Taddeo Gaddi (left of the main altar), and a *glazed terracotta* depicting the *Visitation* from the della Robbia workshop.

VILLONE PUCCINI – Once more open to the public, after being carefully restored, it is a great public park full of trees, situated at the bottom of the hilly area, at the beginning of the roads leading out of the town towards the Abetone and the Porretta pass. It was first laid out by order of Niccolò Puccini as a great landscaped English-type garden, with reconstructed "Classical ruins", in accordance with the fashion of the times. The lake with its little island and "Greek temple" as well as a number of "Gothic relics" are still extant.

SPIRITO SANTO – This church gives his name to the square onto which it faces. It is near the Cathedral and looks like a piece of Baroque Rome transplanted into Tuscany: a main altar designed by Bernini, a great altar-piece by Pietro da Cortona, a carved wooden organ by a Flemish master, rare marble facings; the church was designed first by Tommaso Ramignani in 1647 and initially dedicated to St. Ignatius (as the sponsors where the Jesuit Order).

VILLA DI CELLE – A patrician villa on the Montalese road, surrounded by a park of hoary old oaks and chestnut trees, with a lake and works by some of the best known contemporary artists. The combination of all these elements has produced a unique open-air museum: sculpture, constructions and inventions have been scattered through the wood by Kounellis, Melotti, Karavan and many others over the past years, thanks to the interest in modern art of the owner. Visits have to be booked in advance.

ZOOLOGICAL GARDENS – The Zoo is arranged on the wooded slopes of a hill and along the banks of a little lake. There is quite a large variety of animal species, some of them extremely rare, some kept in a semi-wild state; the Reptile House is particularly interesting.

The 15th century well in Piazza della Sala.

The church of San Paolo; below: the equestrian statue of Giuseppe Garibaldi in the square named after him.

The Hospital of the «Ceppo»; below: details of the enamelled terracotta frieze by the Della Robbia workshop.

The 12th century church of Sant'Andrea.

The fine flank of the church of San Giovanni Fuorcivitas.

THE PROVINCE OF PISTOIA

1. The Pistoia mountain range — 2. Valdinievole.

1. THE PISTOIA MOUNTAIN RANGE

The area known as the Pistoia mountain range comprises a vast area of the Appenines to the north of Pistoia, between the Abetone and the pass of Collina, including the courses of the Ombrone, Lima and Reno rivers. The history of the Range centres on its roads, the oldest of which is the old Roman road that linked Pistoia to Bologna along the valley of the Reno, after which there was a Longobard road that marched to Modena via the Abetone; a number of cross-roads linked these two major routes at various points (the most centrally placed one is the road that runs along the course of the Lima towards Lucca) forming a network of roads controlled through the centuries by Pistoia. Soon, however, the main communication routes that linked the north of the peninsula to the south shifted to other roads and areas and the Pistoia Range only experienced true economic development (due to tourism and a number of industrial activities — chiefly paper-mills and foundries) in the 20th century. Before that and up to very recently the livelihood of the inhabitants of the Pistoia Range depended on the chestnut woods, and the ice and charcoal trade. Along the road leading up to the Abetone, one encounters **San Marcello**, an ancient Free Commune, full of pride in its independence which boasts a wax *Ecce Homo* in its **parish church** by Gaetano Zumbo, but very few other traces of its past. Wooden artifacts and sweet pastry made of chestnut flour are some of its most important products. Nearby is **La Lima**, with its impressive suspension bridge. One proceeds towards the Abetone, along the Modena road and one encounters **Cutigliano**, the seat of important Magistratures during the Middle Ages and Renaissance, the birth-place of poets and soldiers of fortune. The 14th/15th century Praetorian Palace is studded all over its façade with armorial bearings; opposite is the **Marzocco Column** and the **Market loggia**, both built in the Renaissance. From Cutigliano one can reach the Doganaccia skiing fields. Further up, a side-road off to **Rivoreta**, where one can visit a very well-kept Museum of Rural Traditions (**Museo della civiltà contadina**). The **Abetone** was originally a gigantic, hoary old fir- tree that was cut down in 1777, so that the last stretch of the road to Modena could be completed (at an altitude of 1388 metres). Two pyramids were put up on the site in Peter Leopold of Tuscany's and Duke Francesco III of Este's honour. The first skiers arrived at the beginning of the 20th century. Since when the fortunes of the Abetone have depended on snow; 50 kms of ski-slopes, 3 cabin-ways, 6 chair-lifts, a bubble-lift, hotels, restaurants, banks, discotheques... The Abetone was where one of the first and most important skiing-clubs in Italy was founded (1927), it boasts champions like Zeno Colò and Celina Seghi and is full of tourists every sufficiently snowy winter. During the summer, visitors can enjoy excursions among the woods, alpine lakes, myrtle-bushes and rhododendrons.

The road that leads up, via the Collina pass to the Porretta pass (state road Nr. 64, also known as the Leopolda or Porrettana), bypasses **Sambuca**, a castle perched above the road which was contended for centuries by Pistoia, the Visconti family, Florence and the Popes.... Not much is left of the old fortress, crouching at the top of the semi-deserted, silent village, watched over by the severe bulk of the church of St. James (**San Giacomo**) and by the ghost of Selvaggia Vergiolesi, the beautiful, luckless maiden sung to by the Stilnovo Pistoia-born poet, Cino da Pistoia.

2. VALDINIEVOLE

The extensive hilly area west of Pistoia between the Ombrone and Serchio rivers derives its name from the river Nievole that crosses it from one end to the other. Leaving Pistoia in the direction of **Serravalle**, a Medieval fortified burg, placed a'sentry at the top of a high hill, one reaches the valley of the Nievole, where olive groves and vineyards create a verdant tapestry; proceeding downwards, one enters Monsummano.

MONSUMMANO – A well-known shoe-manufacturing centre and watering place, it appears to be divided into two parts: the more

Campo Tizzoro - Overall view.

Abetone - Overall view.

Monsummano Terme - The sanctuary of Santa Maria Fontenuova.

Abetone - The square with the Pyramids recalling the construction of the Modena road, ordered by Pietro Leopoldo of Tuscany and Francesco III d'Este. Below: **Monsummano Terme** - The entrance to the Giusti Grotto.

recently built one down in the plain, the other, more ancient part securely perched on its rocky ridge.

The sanctuary of **Santa Maria Fontenuova**, an elegant Baroque construction from the beginning of the 16th century, overlooks the main square with its statue of Giuseppe Giusti, a poet born in Monsummano. Just outside the town, one can visit the **Giusti Grotto** and the **Parlanti Grotto**, the former a natural and the latter an artificial grotto, where the spa establishments are. Up in **Monsummano Alto**, one can see the picturesque ruins of the fort founded around the beginning of the 11th century. The village appears to be enveloped in splendid isolation: a little cemetery, a few houses around the square in front of the parish church of **San Niccolò** (11th century) which survives intact, surrounded by the town walls, the grassy terrace, beside the church, overlooking the plain, all help to create the impression of a microcosm — a world apart, in which time has stopped. Leaving Monsummano, one returns to the state road Nr. 435.

MONTECATINI

MONTECATINI – An elegant watering place, one of the best known and most visited in Italy, it has been renowned since the Middle Ages for the salutary properties of its waters, as well as for its social life, fine shops and numerous literary, musical, etc. events, organised within its precincts.

The modern church of **Santa Maria Assunta** overlooks the main square, Piazza del Popolo. Shady Viale Verdi and the carefully tended Parco delle Terme separate the tourist- frequented, socially prestigious part (to the west, with luxurious hotels and shops and fashionable haunts) from the quieter, simpler eastern part. The main spa establishments are in the park mentioned above. To name but a few: the **Tettuccio** and the **Excelsior**, built in Liberty style in 1915 and the **Terme Leopoldine**. The backdrop to the whole town is the picturesque hilltop Medieval burg of **Montecatini Alto** with the ruins of the old fortress and a charming little square crowded throughout the summer with multi-coloured coffee-tables.

Proceeding along the 435, one reaches Pescia.

PESCIA

PESCIA – A pretty little town on the banks of the torrent Pescia, it is chiefly renowned for its nursery gardens and flower plantations (mostly carnations), which have given it international repute. A Free Commune since the earliest times, it ranged its loyalties first on the side of Lucca thereafter (early 14th century) it took the Florentine side, achieving considerable importance under the Medici government.

The **Porta Fiorentina**, a spectacular triumphal arch built in 1732 for Giangastone de' Medici leads into the most ancient part with the **Cathedral**, restructured in the Baroque style at the end of the 17th century and flanked by its imposing 1306 bell tower; the Gothic church of **San Francesco** (end of the 13th century) where one can admire a splendid panel — painted by Bonaventura Berlinghieri (1235) — depicting the Saint to whom the church is dedicated; the diminutive oratory of **San Domenico** (14th century) with a fine wooden 13th century *Deposition*. See also today's Town Hall housed in the **Palazzo dei Vicari**, built between the 13th and 14th centuries as well as the elegant Renaissance oratory of the **Madonna di Piè di Piazza** (1447) placed at either end of the long Piazza Mazzini, heart of the town since its earliest times.

Montecatini Terme - The Tettuccio spa establishment; below: the entrance to the Excelsior spa establishment.

Montecatini Alto - Overall view.

Montecatini Terme - The interior of the Tettuccio spa establishment. Below: **Pescia** - The Florentine Gate, built for Giangastone de' Medici in 1732; the Cathedral with its strong bell tower.

LUCCA

Lucca originated as a Roman settlement at the intersection of three consular roads by the Serchio River. In the Middle Ages, fierce rival of Pisa and Florence, it prospered on textile manufacture and trade (i.e., import of Oriental silks). This period (especially the 13th century) was the time of great building activity - numerous churches in the striking style later known as Pisan Lucchese rose all over the city. Except for a few sporadic intervals, Lucca remained an independent republic for five centuries. During the Renaissance period, when banking became one of the city's chief activities, great palaces and mansions were built in and around it. The city's impressive girth of walls date from a later period (16th-17th centuries). In 1799, after having withstood centuries of attempts by the Tuscans to add Lucca's territory to the grandducal domains, Lucca succumbed to the French. Thereafter, it was a principality governed by Elisa Baciocchi, Napoleon's sister, and later a Bourbon possession, before becoming part of the Kingdom of Italy. Two of Italy's greatest composers, Luigi Boccherini and Giacomo Puccini, were born here in the 1800s. Its economic mainstays are agriculture (olive oil) some industry, paper, and tourism. Every two years the *Italian Cartoon & Comics Festival* is held here.

RECOMMENDED ITINERARIES – All of the sights described are inside the city walls. Starting from tree-shaded *Piazza Napoleone* (bordered by a 16th-18th century building, the *Palazzo della Provincia*), cross the adjoining square, Piazza del Giglio, to reach the 12th century church of *San Giovanni* on *Piazza San Giovanni*. Proceeding in the same direction, you come to the **Duomo** on Piazza San Martino. Retrace your steps to Piazza Napoleone, turn right into Via Vittorio Veneto, and continue to *Piazza San Michele*. On the square are two notable buildings, the church of **San Michele in Foro** and, on the righhand corner, *Palazzo Pretorio*, a 16th century porticoed building. Continue along Via Calderia, cross *Piazza del Salvatore*, and take Via Battisti to the church of **San Frediano**. (If, instead, you go left from Piazza del Salvatore into Via Santa Giustina and then take Via Galli Tassi, you come to the **Pinacoteca Nazionale** or National Painting Gallery). After crossing Piazza San Frediano, take *Via Fillungo*, lined with medieval houses and towers, and proceed to the *marketplace* which rises on the site of the *Roman amphitheater*. (This explains its characteristic elliptical shape). From Via Fillungo, go left into Via Sant'Andrea, along which stand 14th century turreted brick buildings, the so-called *Guinigi Houses*. Then, take Via Guinigi, go right on Via Mordini, and continue down Via della Fratta. A bit past Piazza San Francesco is Lucca's major museum, the **Villa Guinigi National Museum**. A walk atop the **city walls** is an excellent way to appreciate their dimensions.

CATHEDRAL – The original 11th-13th century Romanesque building dedicated to St. Martin was rebuilt in the Gothic style during the 14th-15th centuries. Its facade is adorned with impressive Romanesque sculpture.

The facade dates from the first building campaign. The portal sculpture is superb, especially the *Nativity* and *Deposition* of the left portal, both attributed to Nicola Pisano. The interior is a treasurehouse of artworks. To the right of the entrance is a 13th century Lucchese Lombard sculpture depicting *St. Martin and the Beggar*. A painting by Tintoretto (*Last Supper*) adorns the third altar on the righthand side. Many of the most important works are 15th century: a Ghirlandaio altarpiece (sacristy), a mosaic depicting the *Judgment of Solomon* (nave floor), a *statue of St. John the Evangelist* by Jacopo della Quercia, and the most famous of all, Jacopo della Quercia's *Tomb of Ilaria del Carretto* (left transept). Along the left aisle is the *Tempietto del Volto Santo*, crafted by Matteo Civitali in 1498, which contains a much revered 11th-12th century Byzantine *Crucifix*.

SAN MICHELE IN FORO – The facade of this striking 12th-14th century church, typically Pisan Lucchese in style, is topped by an immense statue of *St. Michael*. The *Virgin and Child* on the right corner is by Civitali. Inside the church are various works, including a 13th

Overall view of Lucca with the elegant bell tower of the Cathedral; below: the handsome Pisan façade of San Michele in Foro.

The Market Square (Piazza del Mercato) which occupies the erstwhile Amphitheatre; below, right: the Cathedral.

The Tomb of Ilaria del Carretto, the famous sepulchre by Jacopo della Quercia, in the Cathedral; below: the statue of the Archangel Michael, above the façade of San Michele in Foro.

century wooden *Crucifix* (right transept), a *Virgin and Child* by Andrea della Robbia (right transept), and a Filippino Lippi altarpiece (left transept).

NATIONAL MUSEUM– The museum building is a 17th century palace, *Palazzo Mansi*, which still has much of its original furnishings. The collection, comprising 16th-19th century paintings, contains several fine portraits by Bronzino and Sustermans, two portraits and a scene of *St. Mark freeing a slave* by Tintoretto, *Peter the Hermit before the Venetian Senate* by Veronese, as well as works by Barocci, Andrea del Sarto, Furini, Salvator Rosa, and Schiavone.

SAN FREDIANO – Built between the 12th and 13th centuries, the church has a simple facade adorned with a great mosaic of the *Ascension*. The highlights of the interior are a 12th century Romanesque font with fine reliefs, della Robbia terracottas, and the lavishly-decorated *Cappella Trenta* adorned with sculpture by Jacopo della Quercia.

VILLA GUINIGI NATIONAL MUSEUM – The museum building, the recently-restored 15th century brick **Villa Guinigi**, sports a distinctive porticoed facade. Roman, medieval, and 18th century sculpture adorn the grounds.

Ground floor: Ligurian, Etruscan, and Roman archeology and sculpture of the following periods: Early Christian, Romanesque, Gothic (e.g., a fine Pisan-Lucchese style partition with *Samson and the lion* carved in the 13th century and an *Annunciation* by a follower of Nino Pisano), as well as Renaissance (e.g., *Ecce Homo* by Civitali). Upstairs: carved wood choir stalls, altar frontals, and other wood church fittings of various periods, *portrait of Alessandro dei Medici* by Pontormo, three painted *crucifixes* (12th-13th centuries), 14th-15th century Lucchese school paintings, two Fra Bartolomeo altarpieces, furnishings, textiles, and silver and gold, as well as works by a local 18th century master, Pompeo Batoni.

CITY WALLS – These impressive city walls, erected in the 16th-17th centuries, never served as protection against enemy attack - rather, they were instrumental in preventing the Serchio from flooding and conserving medieval Lucca virtually intact for three hundred years. A pleasant way to tour the city is to walk along the approximately four-km-long tree-shaded avenue which runs around the town.

THE PROVINCE OF LUCCA

1. The Lucca Villas — 2. The Versilia — 3. The Garfagnana.

1. THE LUCCA VILLAS

The wide area to the east of Lucca between the district known as the "six-mile-plain" and the slopes of the Pizzorne hills, was filled with an incredible number of patrician dwellings as from the 16th century. The garden enclosures have subtly altered the landscape, managing however to adapt their verdant structures to the nature of terrain. This phenomenon is most certainly to be linked to the lengthy era of prosperity enjoyed by the merchants of Lucca and coincided with their desire to escape from the city walls and invest their new wealth in land. In the Lucca villas, the representative function overrides all other considerations so that the parks and architecture of these establishments are more sumptuous than in any other part of Tuscany. If one proceeds along state road Nr 435 in the direction of Pescia, one finds a side-road branching off to **Camigliano**, where one can visit **Villa Torrigiani**, which was given its present appearance between the 17th and 18th centuries. A long cypress-avenue and an imposing gate offer an impressive vista. The Baroque statues, the niches, the tiered arches of the façade appear to be a stage-setting, overlooking the vast lawn or manège. All around: the luxuriant fronds of the liriodendron and plane trees of the landscaped English-style part of the garden, restructured during the last century. The Italianate part is off, on the right,

The tall Guinigi Tower soaring above one of the old medieval alleys in the town; below: an avenue along the walls.

The simple façade of San Frediano with the gleaming mosaic panel of the Ascension; below: a section of the imposing old fortifications of the town.

hidden beyond beds of camelias that recall the origins of the name of Camigliano: from camelia, a plant that used to flourish spontaneously in this area. Uphill, one encounters a rectangular pool flanked by lemon-trees; down-hill one finds the "secret garden", with its neatly clipped box hedges and beds, which one enters via a descending double ramp of stairs surrounding a nympheum or water grotto; at the other end of the garden, is the Cavern of the Winds: a dark grotto of spongey stone with niches enclosing statues representing the Winds; above the grotto (that conceals hidden water sprinklers), there is a domed shrine sheltering the statue of Flora. The interior of the villa is a classical example of a patrician residence, beautifully decorated and furnished. A few kilometres northwards, in **Segromigno**, is the **Villa Mansi**, which was built towards the middle of the 17th century. The great park, originally laid out in splendid Baroque style by Juvara with a host of pools, temples and sculptures, has been almost totally re-planned in the 19th century English landscaped style. The nearby extensive grounds of the **Royal Villa** of **Marlia** enjoy the same kind of atmosphere. The villa had been restructured innumerable times since the 16th century before it underwent its radical and final restructuring, by order of Elisa Baciocchi, Napoleon's sister and Grand Duchess of Tuscany (with a court in Lucca), at the beginning of the 19th century. Elisa Baciocchi wished to receive her august guests in a milieu worthy of her rank. Returning to the state road, and proceeding towards Pescia, one encounters the most extravagant and spectacular garden in the Lucca area, the **Villa Garzoni** gardens in **Collodi**. No longer in the "six-mile-plain", but already in the Valdinievole and bound to Lucca by traditional ties, the villa was built upon the remains of a Ghibelline fortress. Well after its transformation into a villa, the building maintained a singular relationship with the village ensconced behind it, inasmuch as it was the sole means of entrance into the burg. Nowadays a road connects Collodi to the valley network, by circumventing the garden walls, but the village, which is arranged fishbone fashion on each side of a main street traversing the burg from end to end, still seems to be nestling up to the mighty back of the "great house" as if it would otherwise slither downhill. The garden, arranged on a slope and off-centre compared with the villa, can be embraced in its totality at a single glance. This theatrical immediacy must have appealed to the pride-full soul of Romano Garzoni, who planned the whole complex in the 17th century. An extensive parterre section arranged around two large circular pools, statues of rural and mythological personalities, box hedges clipped into fanciful shapes, multicoloured flower-beds and, further up, the plumey fronds of palms and cypresses. An elegant series of crossed levels mounts up the hill to the upper terraces. On the first, a rocky grotto in which water spouts from unexpected jets. A staircase waterfall creates extraordinary, glistening transparency effects right up to the two statues representing rivers and the colossal statue of Fame, behind which one can visit the Baths, which are of the Roman type, in which the two sexes could bathe unseen by each other, separated by a screen through which they could, however, converse to the strains of music played by a chamber orchestra, concealed behind another screen. Next door to the villa is a charming labyrinth; from an overhead bridge, by means of strategically placed taps one could make it even more difficult for the hapless prisoners of the maze to get out of the box hedges, which can be a more complicated task than one would expect (the taps are nowadays generally disconnected). Beside the maze is a dense bamboo thicket, a rarity in those days, giving one some idea of the widespread taste for botanical collector's pieces. A visit to the Villa can be rewarding, as it offers an interesting insight into a Baroque world (which is Rococò in the summer apartments) where all the furnishings, the paintings and the beautiful kitchens breathe 17th century. Returning down to the parterre beds, one passes a charming little green theatre. Across the road from the gardens, is the modern **Pinocchio Park** (for children) which is a reconstruction of the fairy-tale world inhabited by the famous wooden puppet created by Carlo Collodi, whose pen-name and family had their origins in the village.

2. THE VERSILIA

The wide plain that stretches from the Apuan hills to the sea, now so densely populated and scattered all over with well-known sea-side resorts, used to belong to the district of the Vicar of Pietrasanta, which used to be the most important centre of the area.

VIAREGGIO – A wide beach, pine-woods, an excellent tourist organisation, the harbour, the climate and the neighbouring mountains explain the irresistible economic boom enjoyed by the little town in the course of this century of mass holidays at manageable costs. The

Marlia - The Lemon-tree Garden in the park of the Royal Villa.

Collodi - Monument to Pinocchio, by Emilio Greco (1956) in the park dedicated to the famous puppet from the story by Carlo Lorenzini.

Marlia - The pool in the Lemon-tree Garden and (below, left) the semi-circular pool in the park of the Royal Villa. Below, right: **Collodi** - The gardens of Villa Garzoni.

Collodi - Reconstruction of the Whale of Pinocchio.

famous procession of allegorical carts that takes place during Carnival, as well as a renowned summertime literary festival add to the attractions of the place.

Up to the 12th century, not only was there no trace of Viareggio, but the terrain on which it rose was partly under water and partly marshy swamp-land. For centuries, the place remained deserted, except for a small castle, manned by troops from the town of Lucca, who decided to construct a small harbour for their trade-ships. The woods and marshes were rife with malaria which managed to withstand repeated and prolonged land reclamation attempts. The battle was only won during the Renaissance: in the 16th century, Lucca built a number of buildings nearer to the sea-board, with depôts, a fine watch tower (the **Matilda Tower**), an inn, the first of a long series: the *Grande Hostaria*. In 1559, the fishermen got their church of San Pietro, then the church of **Santissima Annunziata** was built next to the tower. Meanwhile the harbour expanded (not excessively, so as not to arouse the hostility of nearby Livorno, controlled by the powerful and aggressive Florentines). Malaria and swamp-land were only finally vanquished in the 18th century, thanks to considerable technical and economic efforts. The first patrician villas were built and the population grew together with the economic fortunes of the place, in the following century and along came tree-lined avenues, carriages and, after the 1870s, Liberty-style: the Margherita theatre and the Balena bathing establishment were built (to name but a few of the buildings that have preserved their original appearance).

South of Viareggio and founded even more recently, is **Torre del Lago**, an agricultural centre and holiday resort. From the village, a shady lime-tree avenue leads down to the **lake of Massaciuccoli**, where one can visit **Giacomo Puccini's villa**. The villa still possesses the charm of a slightly Liberty-style, turn of the century dwelling, that its present status as museum has not quite managed to erase: a lived-in, intimate feeling. Everything has been left as it was: Puccini's clothes, his bed, his glasses, his music-sheets, the piano at which the great composer composed his most loved operas, from *Bohème* to *Tosca* to *Turandot*. Not even his guns are missing: he used to go and stand in a barrel with one of his guns and wait for water-fowl to flutter in his direction, whenever he got weary of sitting at his piano. The lake, surrounded by a dream-like landscape full of water-rushes and shimmering reflections, its water teaming with tench and pike, is all that remains of the immense swamp-land between the lower reaches of the Arno and Serchio rivers. A delightful spot, that Puccini loved so much, that he asked to be buried there. His tomb (1924) is in the villa chapel. It seems unnecessary to mention that Torre del Lago is a must for opera-fans, who are even further attracted to the place by the summer Puccini Festival that takes place every year, drawing hundreds of visitors from all over the world to enjoy the balmy lake shore. The coast north of Viareggio is one long, uninterrupted succession of little seaside resorts that can only be distinguished from one another by their names: **Lido di Camaiore, Focette, Marina di Pietrasanta, Forte dei Marmi, Cinquale**. The most important one is Forte dei Marmi, which derives its name from a fortress, commissioned by Leopold II in 1788, which is still the centre of the town — and from the marble quarried in the neighbouring Apuan hills, which for a certain period, used to be loaded onto transport craft in the harbour. Among the island towns, just a short way away from Forte de' Marmi is **Pietrasanta**. The ancient burg, still renowned for its marble processing yards, was founded in 1255 by Guiscardo Pietrasanta, podestà of Lucca. The most important buildings comprise the **Cathedral** (13/14th cent.), with its fine marble façade and a large number of admirable statues inside — as well as the church of **Sant'Agostino** (Gothic, 14th cent.). In nearby **Valdicastello** is the birth place of Giosuè Carducci, the poet. Yet further inland, at the feet of the Apuan hills, one finds **Camaiore**, a considerable agricultural centre; its 13th century Romanesque **Collegiata** is very beautiful and its **Museo d'arte sacra** (Museum of Religious Art) as well as the church of the 11th century Benedictine **Abbey** are both fascinating.

3. THE GARFAGNANA

This itinerary runs along the upper and middle reaches of the Serchio valley, wending through the Appenines north of Lucca. The area was given the name of Garfagnana in the Middle Ages; it was ruled over by Lucca until the middle of the 14th century, then it was divided up among the Florentines, the Lucchese and the Malaspina family. In the 15th century, part of the area was taken over by the Este family, who despatched Ludovico Ariosto there as Governor. It is a

Viareggio - The jetty.

Torre del Lago - The monument to Giacomo Puccini; below: the Lake of Massaciuccoli.

Viareggio - A section of the esplanade that winds past all the bathing establishments. Below: **Forte dei Marmi** - The little quay.

land of ancient farming and pastoral traditions with a richly varied landscape: lush and densely cultivated in the low-lying areas and starkly desolate and wild on the upper ridges of the Apuan and Appenine hills. One proceeds along state road Nr. 12 until **Bagni di Lucca**. The fortunes of the place known at the time as Bagni di Corsena started thriving in the 11th century under the rule of Matilda of Tuscany, but its lime-sulphate springs were already known in Roman times. One returns to the Serchio river and proceeds, right, along its banks until one reaches Barga.

BARGA

BARGA – The most important centre in the central reaches of the Serchio valley. Its ancient streets, of Longobard origin, twine around a hilltop. The Barga Opera Festival attracts hundreds of opera fans every year.

The **Cathedral** is the most important building: founded in the 11th century and finally completed in the 14th. A lovely, plain travertine façade and a battlemented bell tower; inside, a nave and two side aisles, a Lucchese School 12th century sculpted pulpit, works by the Della Robbia workshop in the chapel of the Sacrement, a 15th century *Crucifix* and golden artifacts in the Treasury (Tesoro). Next door, one can admire the **Praetorian Palace** with the **Podestà's loggia**. In Piazza del Comune, one finds the **Loggia of the Market** and the **Palace of the Commune**, both 16th century. 4 kms. beyond Barga one comes to **Castelvecchio Pascoli**, where one can visit the house in which the poet Giovanni Pascoli (1855-1912) composed his *Songs of Castelvecchio*. From Pascoli's hamlet, one takes the road down to the valley floor again and, after crossing the river, one reaches Gallicano from where one can get onto the road leading up to the Apuan hills. On ones right one encounters the Hermitage of Calomini (**Eremo di Calomini**), a picturesque monastery partially dug out of the rocky mountainside. Not far from **Fornovolasco** one encounters the **Grotto of the Wind** (del Vento) surrounded by the magnificent Apuan landscape: a richly sedimented limestone cave, with underground streams and waterfalls. Returning to the central route, one proceeds northward until one reaches Castelnuovo di Garfagnana.

CASTELNUOVO DI GARFAGNANA

CASTELNUOVO DI GARFAGNANA – The chief town of the Garfagnana district proper, it is situated at the point in which the Turrite Secca flows into the Serchio. It owes its importance to the Este family who decided, in the 15th century, to use the town as the reference point of their various estates in the area.

Between 1522 and 1525 the **Rocca** (Fortress) was the residence of Ludovico Ariosto, the author of the magnificent poem *Orlando Furioso*, when he was sent against his will by his patron to be Governor in Garfagnana. The **Cathedral** has a 16th century appearance and contains an *Assumption* by Santi di Tito. See also the 17th century **Capucin Monastery** and the 18th century **Notarie's Archives**.

A magnificent road leaves Castelnuovo and winds dizzily up to the Radici pass, on its way towards Pievepelago. As one proceeds along it, one meets **Pieve Fosciana** with its 14th century parish church and **Castiglione di Garfagnana**, a fortified Lucchese burg, founded in the 14th century, where one can visit a number of interesting churches. After the pass, a road off right leads towards **San Pellegrino in Alpe**, an ancient pilgrims' hospice near the famous **Sanctuary**, which is supposed to have been founded in the 7th century by a son of the King of Scotland who withdrew to these mountains to spend the rest of his days in penance. Inside the Sanctuary, one can admire a beautiful shrine designed by Matteo Civitali. In the **Ethnographic Museum**, next door, interesting farming utensils, domestic furnishings, and other equipment used in everyday life by the farming communities in the Garfagnana.

MASSA and CARRARA

MASSA – It was founded on the banks of the river Frigido, at the foot of a hill crowned by an ancient fortress. Together with Carrara, which shares its position as capital of a province, it is a flourishing marble industry centre, dependant on the exploitation of the quarries in the nearby Apuan hills, the towering cliffs of which bestride the horizon

Borgo a Mozzano - The Devil's Bridge.

Massa - The Cathedral; below: the church of San Rocco outside the centre of the town.

Marina di Massa - A stretch of beach with the Apuan Alps in the background. Below: **Massa** - The Cybo-Malaspina Palace.

all around, their gleaming whiteness recalling the eternal snows. Between the 15th and 18th centuries it was ruled over by the Malaspina and Cybo Malaspina, thereafter it became part of the Este domains when a Cybo married an Este. It was occupied by the French army in 1796 and was included in the Principality of Lucca under Elisa Bonaparte Baciocchi. After the Congress of Vienna (1815) it was restored to the Este family, under whose sway it remained until 1859, when it was annexed by the Kingdom of Sardinia. The 16th century part of the town is arranged around Piazza degli Aranci, where one finds the handsome **Palazzo Cybo Malaspina** (16th-17th cents.), now used as the prefecture (police); the fine inner loggiaed courtyard was designed in the 17th century, whereas the colourful façade with its lively design was added in 1701. Not far away is the Cathedral, which was founded in the 14th century but was restructured on various occasions in successive centuries (the interior is Baroque and the façade was added during the first half of this century). In the *Chapel of the Blessed Sacrament* (the last one on the right) there are the remains of a Pinturicchio fresco depicting the *Virgin*, a triptych by the Lippi Circle and a 16th cent. terracotta *Nativity* group. In the crypt, one can visit the monumental sepulchres of the Cybo Malaspina. The **Fortress** overlooking the town consists of a Medieval section, linked by a loggia to the palace built by order of the Malaspina family during the 15th and 16th centuries, as their residence. Nearby, is the church of **San Rocco**, where one can admire a *Crucifix* attributed to Michelangelo in his youth.

CARRARA – It is the headquarters of some of the most important industrial plants in the marble processing field, thanks to the enormous supply of the stone available in the neighbouring quarries of the Apuan hills, beneath which the town nestles. Its economy and history are linked to those of nearby Massa. Carrara shared Massa's destinies, belonging first to the Malaspina and Cybo Malaspina families (15th to 18th cents.) then to the Este, the French and Elisa Bonaparte Baciocchi (18th-19th cents.) then to the Este family again (after 1815) and finally to the Kingdom of Sardinia (1859). Most of its buildings are modern, but there are a number, which are of considerable historical and artistic interest, the most important one being the **Cathedral**, an 11th- 14th cent. Romanesque-Gothic structure with a Pisan-type horizontally banded, two-coloured marble façade with 12th century blind arches on the lower section and a loggia and superb, richly carved rose-window on the upper section. The Romanesque portal on the right flank, the apse with its loggia and the second half of the 13th century belltower are very fine as well. The restored interior has an austere nave divided from the side-aisles by columns with very interesting capitals. In the right aisle, see a beautiful sculpted 14th century *Angel and Virgin Annunciate*; the choir is surrounded by a very fine 16th century marble enclosure by Francesco Bergamini; both the 16th century finely carved marble altar as well as the multicoloured marble pulpit of the same period are worthy of note. In the left aisle see a 14th century marble altarpiece with a *Madonna and Saints*. The neighbouring *baptistery* contains a fine 16th century baptismal font. In the square, right of the church, is a 16th century fountain by Baccio Bandinelli, with the statue of Andrea Doria represented as Neptune. Handsome 17th century patrician mansions are to be seen around the nearby Piazza Alberica and not far away one sees the 16th century **Cybo Malaspina Palace**, nowadays the headquarters of the **Academy of Fine Arts**. In the courtyard, there is a rare archaeological find: a Roman shrine removed from the Fantiscritti quarry, a few miles away, known as the **Aedicula of Fantiscritti**. Among the quarries which are still being exploited and can be visited in the vicinity of Carrara (such as the quarries of Colonnata and Ravaccione), the quarry of *Fantiscritti* can be reached by climbing up the narrow bends leading up to the beginning of the **Fantiscritti canal**, where the quarrying operations are in full swing against a highly spectacular and unusual backdrop.

Massa - The Crucifix attributed to Michelangelo, as a young man, in the church of San Rocco.

Carrara - 16th century fountain, by Bandinelli, with the statue of Andrea Doria, as Neptune; in the background the side of the Cathedral and the bell tower.

Carrara - Piazza Alberica; below: an Apuan marble quarry, with the marble block slide or chute; the Fantiscritti bridge.

THE PROVINCE OF MASSA

1. THE LUNIGIANA

Proceeding northwards along the Via Aurelia, one encounters a road leading off left, towards Luni, the ancient chief town of the Lunigiana. Notwithstanding its many fascinating aspects, the latter is one of the least known and visited parts of Italy. The Lunigiana runs roughly from Pontremoli to Aulla, stretching along the course of the Magra river. It is an area possessing its own distinctive customs and traditions derived from the fact that it is a kind of melting pot in which Aemilian, Tuscan and Ligurian cultures have met and blended. Its war-ridden history has given it a whole series of well-fortified settlements strenuously defended throughout the many visits payed over the centuries by foreign invaders.

Fosdinovo - View with the Castle.
Pontremoli - View with the Tower of the Great Bell (Campanone).

LUNI – An ancient Roman colony, founded in 177 B.C., in the region it gave its name to; it flourished until around the 4th century, when its decline set in, chiefly because of malaria epidemics and repeated onslaughts by the Longobards, the Normans and most of all by the Saracens.

The erstwhile splendour of the Roman town can be divined in what remains of the forum, where one finds the ruins of two temples and the imposing relics of an amphitheatre (1st cent B.C.?). The **Archaeological Museum** contains various pieces that have been dug up in the area.

Proceeding along the Aurelia, one reaches **Sarzana**, an ancient burg fortified by the Genoese, possessing a 13th century **Cathedral** crouching beneath the **Fortress of Sarzanello**. From Sarzana, a road leads-up right, towards the Apuan hills and arrives at **Fosdinovo**, a picturesque little village, the foundation date and origin of whose name is still shrouded in mystery. It boasts a superb 14th century **castle**, the gigantic bulk of which dwarfs the rest of the constructions beneath it. At Sarzana one leaves the Aurelia and takes state road Nr. 62, which climbs up towards the Appennines along the course of the river Magra. After a short while, one gets to **Aulla**. The little town is situated at the confluence of the Aulella with the Magra. Its **parish church** was built on the site of the great and extremely ancient Abbey of San Caprasio, which belonged to the Malaspina family and then became the property of the Genoese Centurione family. The latter were responsible for the construction of the **Brunella** fortress, overlooking the medieval burg and the valley below. The road continues through increasingly thickly forested country, until one reaches Villafranca in Lunigiana, where one can admire the romantic ruins of **Castello Malaspina** and the 16th century church of **San Francesco**. Proceeding along road Nr. 62, one encounters Filattiera, another Medieval burg that has preserved its former appearance, with a **castle** and the little church of **San Giorgio**; in the cemetery, one can see the remains of an ancient Romanesque parish church containing a prehistoric menhir. The road continues and, at the end of the valley, where the hill-sides narrow-in, leading up to the Cisa pass, one comes to Pontremoli.

PONTREMOLI – The most important town in the Lunigiana, has its ancient nucleus situated at the confluence of the Verde with the Magra.

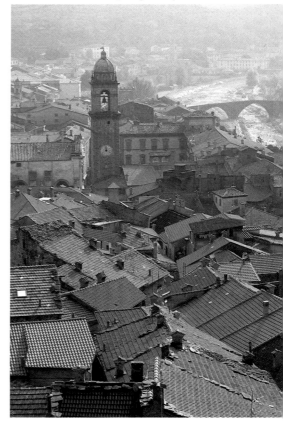

One of the main posting stations along the Via Francigena, it fought bitterly and at length against the Malaspina throughout the Middle Ages; it fell under the sway of Milan between the 14th and 17th centuries; later on it was annexed by the Grand Duchy of Tuscany and by the Dukedom of Parma. It boasts a long tradition of bookstalls and consequently instituted the Bancarella (Bookstall) Literary Festival. Its **Cathedral** is Baroque, with a sculpted bronze door; the church of **San Francesco** contains a *Madonna and Child*, by Agostino di Duccio (15th century) above the second altar on the left; interesting remains of the ancient fortifications (walls, towers, bastions), which include the Tower of the Great Bell (**torre del Campanone**), once part of the fortress built by order of Castruccio Castracani. Inside the **Castle**, at the top of a hill, is the Civic **Archaeological Museum**, which is full of fascinating finds from all over the Lunigiana. Just outside the town is the church of **Santissima Annunziata**, a 16th century church containing a little shrine by Sansovino (1527).

Luni - The imposing remains of the Amphitheatre (probably of the 1st century b.C.). Below: **Pontremoli** - View of the town.

PISA

Pisa, an important port from Roman times, ranked as one of the great Mediterranean sea republics throughout the Middle Ages. In the 11th century, it wrested control of Sardinia, the start of a political and artistic influence not to be relinquished for centuries. Some of the great wealth the city accumulated between the 11th and 13th centuries was lavished on gigantic building projects such as the Campo dei Miracoli religious complex, including their sculptural decoration commissioned from masters such as Nino Pisano (12th century) and Giovanni Pisano (13th century). In 1284, however, Pisa suffered a terrible defeat at the hands of the Genoese in the sea battle of Meloria. The results were political and economic decline and inevitably (from 1406 on) complete dependence on Florence. Under the Medici granddukes, however, recovery was swift (at least economically, due to enlarging of the port, and, culturally, after the University of Pisa was opened). The city, heavily bombed in World War II, was painstakingly restored so that virtually all of its artistic-historical heritage has come down to us.

RECOMMENDED ITINERARIES – 1st ITINERARY: Pisa's great monumental center is the **Campo dei Miracoli** with a host of monuments: **Baptistry**, **Cathedral**, **Leaning Tower**, **Camposanto**, and the *Museo delle Sinopie*, housed in what was once a hospital, the *Spedale di Papa Alessandro*. Next, take *Via Santa Maria*, along which are the *Natural History Museum and Domus Galilaeana*). At the intersection with the *Lungarni*, turn right, cross the river at Ponte Solferino. On your left is **Santa Maria della Spina**, while if you proceed down Lungarno Sonnino you soon come out at **San Paolo a Ripa d'Arno**.

2nd ITINERARY: **Palazzo dei Cavalieri** and **Santo Stefano** are both situated in **Piazza dei Cavalieri**. Take Via dei Consoli del Mare that leads into Piazza Martiri della Libertà (church of **Santa Caterina**). From the square continue along Via San Lorenzo, turn left into Via Berlinghieri, and go straight ahead to the church of **San Francesco** on the square of the same name. Go down Via Sighieri and Via Santa Bibbiana to the *Lungarno Mediceo*. On the left you come to the **National Museum**, while if you go right you soon reach *Ponte di Mezzo*. On medieval *Borgo Stretto* to the right is the Romanesque-Gothic church of *San Michele in Borgo*. Crossing the Arno, you come out in Piazza XX Settembre. On the corner is a Gothic palace, *Palazzo Gambacorti*, which faces the 17th century *Loggia di Banchi*. Lungarno Galilei on the left leads to the 13th century church of *Santo Sepolcro*.

1st ITINERARY

CAMPO DEI MIRACOLI – The buildings on this grassy square (actually Pisa's Piazza del Duomo) constitute one of the foremost complexes of medieval religious architecture. Despite the fact that the buildings date from different periods (11th to 14th century), the impression they convey is of utter stylistic harmony.

BAPTISTRY – The original project drawn up by Diotisalvi around the middle of the 12th century was altered in the course of the next one hundred years by such master architects as Nicola and Giovanni Pisano.

The circular building faced in striped marble is divided into three horizontal registers decorated by arch and gable motifs. A partitioned tile roof surmounts the building. Inside is a masterpiece of medieval sculpture, Nicola Pisano's carved *pulpit*. The reliefs adorning the six sides executed in a monumental, very Classical style represent *scenes from the life of Christ*. The baptismal font is a 13th century masterpiece by Guido da Como.

CATHEDRAL – Although ground was broken in 1064, construction continued well into the 13th century. The tomb of its first architect, Buscheto, is visible at the first arch on the left side of the facade. One of the foremost examples of Pisan Romanesque, the building has all the

The Baptistery; below: the pulpit by Nicola Pisano in the Baptistery; opposite: map of the town and the so-called Field of Miracles (Campo dei Miracoli).

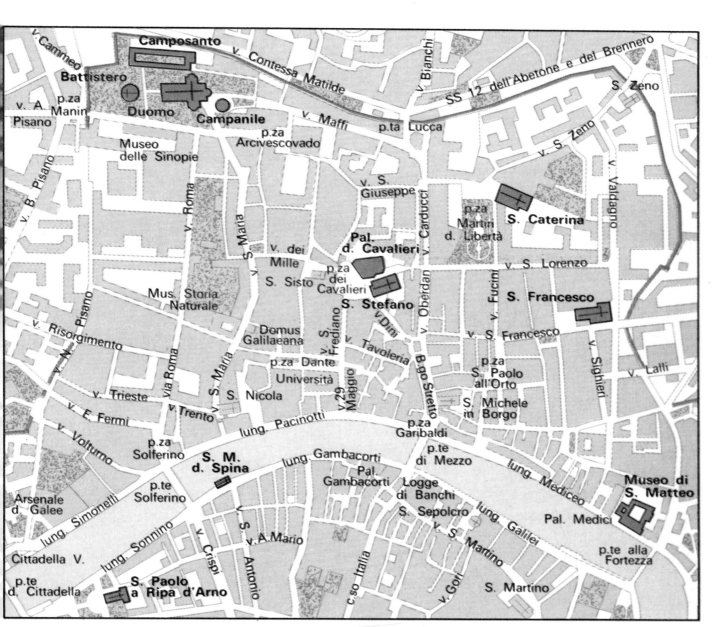

typical features of this style: blind arch motifs, inlay patterns, and ornamental sculpture.

The facade *doors* date from the 16th century when they were put in to replace Bonanno's originals of 1186 that had been destroyed in a fire. All that is left of Bonanno's work is the *Porta di San Ranieri*, the door to the right transept. Dated 1180, it is composed of twenty bronze panels sculpted in a simple, vigorous style. Inside are several noteworthy sights, among them Giovanni Pisano's remarkable carved *pulpit* with *New Testament scenes* in the nave (c. 1310). At the crossing hangs a lighting fixture, the so-called *Galileo's Lamp,* which supposedly sparked the great Pisan scientist's insight into the movement of the pendulum. Other highlights are: Tino di Camaino's *Tomb of Harry VII* (right transept), the great apse mosaic depicting *Christ between the Virgin and St. John the Baptist* (the figure of *St. John* has been attributed to Cimabue), and the sensitive *St. Agnes* by Andrea del Sarto (righthand column in the choir). In the *Treasury* (enter from the Sacristy) are some noteworthy objects, especially reliquaries, and Giovanni Pisano's celebrated *statue of the Virgin* carved out of ivory (late 1200s).

LEANING TOWER – Construction of the belltower, the symbol of Pisa throughout the world, was begun in 1173, possibly under the supervision of Bonanno, and completed two centuries later. It stands 60 meters tall and is inclined 5 meters off perpendicular. Its characteristic inclination is not a recent phenomenom, having begun almost as soon as work on the project got underway (probably due to land slippage, a common phenomenon in Pisan territory). However, the fact that it shows no sign of diminishing has prompted the city to sponsor studies aimed at stabilizing the situation. So far, despite the efforts of engineers and architects all over the world, no solution has been found.

CAMPOSANTO – The wall along the north side of the Campo dei Miracoli belongs to the cemetery (*Camposanto* in Italian). The great *tabernacle* adorning the main portal is by a follower of Giovanni Pisano. The building was begun in 1277 around a famous relic, i.e., earth from the Calvary brought from the Holy Land by the Pisan navy in the 1200s. Destroyed by bombs in 1944, it was restored and its sinopias put on display in a special museum (south side of the square). The interior, which looks like any quiet Gothic cloister, is nevertheless a treasurehouse of art masterpieces. Under the portico are Roman and Early Christian works (including the renowned *Phaedra Sarcophagus* dating from the 2nd century A.D.), inscriptions, plus medieval sculpture and frescoes (many of which in poor condition) painted by masters such as Benozzo Gozzoli, Taddeo Gaddi, and Piero di Puccio. In the next room are the celebrated frescoes depicting the *Triumph of Death,* the *Last Judgment, Hell,* and *scenes of life in an Anacorete monastery.* Art historians are split over the attribution: Traini or Orcagna. The *altar of St. Ranieri* in the nearby *Cappella Ammannati* is adorned with reliefs by Tino di Camaino.

SANTA MARIA DELLA SPINA – This tiny jewel of Gothic architecture (dated 1323) was named after a relic donated by a Pisan merchant. The relic, a thorn (*spina*) from Christ's crown is preserved in a 16th century tabernacle which, along with sculpture by Tommaso Pisano, adorns the interior. The building, moved here from its original location right on the water to protect it from floods, is embellished with sculptural decoration executed by followers of Giovanni Pisano.

SAN PAOLO A RIPA D'ARNO – Founded in the 9th century, the church was rebuilt in the Romanesque style and subsequently remodeled over the centuries. Its typical Pisan Romanesque facade features blind arches and arcading. The interior has a single-aisle plan. The capitals atop the granite columns lining the nave are original. The most interesting features are: a tomb (*Tomba di Burgundio*), made from a Roman sarcophagus (right aisle), a 14th century *Virgin and Child* by Turino Vanni, and a 14th century stained glass window with a *scene of*

The interior of the Cathedral; below: the chandelier known as Galileo's lamp.

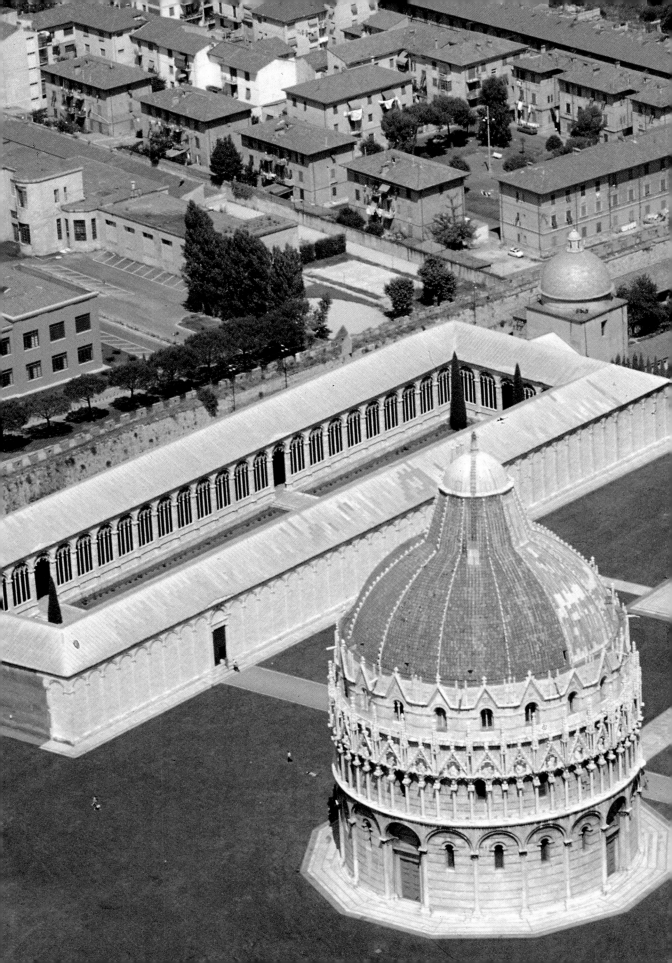

Flank and apse of the Cathedral; right: the Bell Tower or
«Leaning Tower» of world-wide fame.

The outer wall of the great Cemetery (Camposanto); below:
the interior, with its tranquil aspect of a Gothic cloister.

Christ and the Apostles (apse). Detached from the main building is the *Cappella di Sant'Agata*, a 12th century brick structure with an unusual pyramid-shaped cusp roof.

2nd ITINERARY

PIAZZA DEI CAVALIERI – Gothic buildings surrounded this square, the site of the forum of Roman Pisa, until it was rebuilt by Cosimo I dei Medici in the 16th century. One of the famous sights is the *Torre dei Gualandi*, now incorporated into a 16th century palace, *Palazzo dell'Orologio*, where Count Ugolino was left to starve to death (as recounted by Dante in the *Divine Comedy*). Vasari was commissioned by Cosimo to build *Palazzo dei Cavalieri*, which sports a distinctive facade of graffiti patterns. Originally the headquarters of the Order of the Knights of St. Stephan, it is now the Scuola Normale Superiore, Italy's finest university. Vasari also designed the church of *Santo Stefano* adorned with war trophies belonging to the order, Tuscan Mannerist paintings, and a *reliquary-bust* by Donatello.

SANTA CATERINA – Built in the 13th century, the church sports a fine Pisan Romanesque facade. Among the notable artworks displayed inside are: *Triumph of St. Thomas*, attributed to Francesco Traini or Lippo Memmi, the *Tomb of Bishop Saltarelli* by Nino Pisano, and an *Annunciation* group (the *Angel Gabriel* and the *Virgin Annunciate*) also by Nino Pisano.

SAN FRANCESCO – The architect who designed the Camposanto, Giovanni di Simone, also worked on this simple brick church. Inside are interesting 14th century paintings: a *St. Francis* by Santi di Tito, frescoes by Taddeo di Bartolo in the sacristy, and frescoes by Niccolò di Pietro Gerini in the *Sala del Capitolo*.

SAN MATTEO NATIONAL MUSEUM – The collection, begun in the 18th century, is displayed in a lovely old Benedictine monastery.

The exhibits in the first four rooms date mainly from the Roman and Medieval periods. Celebrated sculptures by Giovanni Pisano (*Dancers*, *Female Saint with a Reliquary*, and the *Madonna di Arrigo*) are displayed in Rooms V and VI. A perfect blend of Gothic and Classical elements, they date from the 13th century. Other highlights include: *St. Dominick* by Traini (Room VI), two *Crucifixes* by Giunta Pisano (Rooms VI and XX), illuminated manuscripts (*Treasury* and Room XXIII), a *Virgin and Child* by Simone Martini and the renowned *Madonna del Latte* by Nino Pisano (Room XXI), as well as Masaccio's *St. Paul* (Room XXIV). In addition, there are tapestries (Room XXIII) and works by Giovanni da Milano, Antonio del Ghirlandaio, and others.

Madonna and Child, by Giovanni Pisano, in the Museum of the Cathedral (Museo dell'Opera del Duomo); below: the façade of the 12th century church of Santa Caterina.

THE ENVIRONS OF PISA

1. SAN PIETRO A GRADO — SAN ROSSORE.

Leaving Pisa, by the road that follows the course of the Arno towards the sea, one turns left in the direction of San Pietro.

SAN PIETRO A GRADO – One of the most ancient Early Christian basilicas in Italy, it was founded, according to the legend, by St. Peter himself when he halted there on his way to Rome.

Left: Santa Maria della Spina; right: San Paolo a Ripa d'Arno; below: the fine Knights' Palace (Palazzo dei Cavalieri), by Vasari, headquarters of the Scuola Normale Superiore di Pisa.

The Roman locality of *Gradus*, now at some distance from the coast, used to be a sea-town. The silting-up and the natural accumulation of flotsam transported by the Arno have transformed the surrounding countryside into fertile land. In actual fact, excavations carried out inside the church have revealed that the earliest construction on the site took place in the late Roman imperial era. The existing church, a typical example of Pisan Romanesque architecture, was built between the 10th and 11th centuries, although it has been restructured several times over the following centuries, mostly because of the frequent floods. Many of the architectural elements employed inside came from preexisting Roman edifices: such as the columns, for instance. The frescoes along the main nave are 14th century, attributed to the Lucchese painter, Deodato Orlandi: they depict, on three levels, one above the other: *Portraits of Popes*, *Episodes from the life of St. Peter* and the *Heavenly City*.

If one re-crosses the Arno river, one enters the vast estate of **San Rossore**, which stretches northwards, along the right bank of the river, to the sea. Its name derives from the Christian martyr Lussorio, who was persecuted under the rule of Diocletian and is venerated in Pisa. A little church dedicated to Lussorio (later Rossore) was founded in this very area. The parkland, with its pine-forests, was one of the most loved estates of the Medici, Hapsburg-Lorraine and Savoy families. The Hapsburg-Lorraine family, with the object of keeping to the tradition that established that San Rossore had to be full of wild animals, let a herd of dromedaries loose in the park (the last survivors were exterminated by the Nazis, when they occupied the estate during World War II); the estate today is part of the amenities placed at the disposal of the President of the Republic of Italy and is about to become a National Park; it still contains a large number of wild animals, such as deer, wild boar, squirrels, etc. as well as a wide range of rare and protected botanical species.

MUSEUM OF SAN MATTEO - St. Sebastian and St. Roch, by Ghirlandaio.

San Rossore - The entrance into the Estate; below: an avenue within the vast hunting park.

THE PROVINCE OF PISA

1. Certosa di Calci, Vico Pisano, San Giuliano Terme — 2. San Miniato — 3. Volterra.

1. CERTOSA DI CALCI, VICO PISANO, SAN GIULIANO TERME

Leaving Pisa, one follows the state road Nr. 67 in the direction of Empoli and Florence; at Navacchio, one turns left, crossing the Arno river before one reaches **Caprona**, an ancient village of stone-quarriers. Continuing along the same road, one reaches the foot of Monte Pisano, a group of hills that separate the Pisan from the Lucchese territories. Valgraziosa, one of the many valleys of the Monte Pisano area contains a little village, renowned since the earliest times for the production of lime, which is extracted from the numerous limestone quarries in the area; the product (lime=calce) has given the little burg its name: **Calci**, which gained notoriety by despatching its lime down the Arno to the sea, from where it reached every port on the Mediterranean. The beautiful 11th century Pisan church, in the centre of the village, possesses an elegant façade. Not far from the village, one comes to the Chartreuse.

CERTOSA DI CALCI (Chartreuse of Calci) – The complex was founded in 1366 by Pietro Mirante della Vergine and construction work continued on it for about four hundred years, producing the magnificent results that have survived to this day.

The building, of enormous proportions, belongs nowadays to the State. It is surrounded by orchards and olive-groves, which used to belong to the Abbey. The single-naved *church* is divided into a monks section (towards the altar) and a lay congregation's section (near the doorway) by a wooden screen. The wooden choir stalls are 15th century, whereas the frescoes and decorative elements were added in the 17th century. Next to the church, one encounters a series of small chapels which were used by individual monks (generally cadet sons of patrician families, who would join the community in the abbey accompanied by their servants and household). The cloisters are extremely elegant and very evocative; one of the enclosures contains a small patch of ground which was used as the burial place of the monks (the cemetery was never widened, but was dug deeper and deeper into the ground, one body being buried on top of the other). Other places of great interest include the

The entrance to the Museum of San Matteo.

MUSEUM OF SAN MATTEO - The so-called Madonna of the Milk, by Nino Pisano; below: St. Paul, by Masaccio.

San Pietro a Grado - The Early Christian basilica, one of the most ancient churches in Italy; below: the interior.

105

Refectory, the unusual cells, each one possessing its own garden, the Chapter Rooms and the Grand Ducal Room, in the visitors wing, which had been set aside for the specific use of the Lords of Tuscany who visited the place frequently.

From Calci a charming road climbs up the Monte Pisano until one reaches Buti, from where one proceeds downwards to **Vicopisano**. The village is situated at the top of a hill in a particularly picturesque position. The many rulers who occupied these territories have all left their mark over the centuries specially as regards the successive fortifications that have been built around the town (in the 15th century, even Brunelleschi worked on them). *Brunelleschi's tower* is the most important among the many defensive structures; see also the *Tower of the Four Gates*; the centre of the town is Piazza fra' Domenico Cavalca, dedicated to a 13th century monk who compiled a history of the lives of the Saints; the **parish church** is a Pisan Romanesque building; the **Praetorian Palace** was built in the 14th/15th centuries, and is, as usual, covered all over with crests and armorial bearings. On the other side of Monte Pisano is San Giuliano.

SAN GIULIANO TERME

SAN GIULIANO TERME – A watering place known until not so long ago as Bagni di San Giuliano, which has been famous since Roman times for the curative properties of its waters.

The Romans knew it as the site of the "aquae pisanae", mentioned by Pliny the Elder, and used to travel along the Via Aemilia-Scauri, towards Luni, to get to it. It also derives a certain amount of fame from the neighbouring marble quarries. Its springs, during the Middle Ages, were squabbled over by Pisa and Lucca and all its bathing establishments were destroyed by the Florentines in the 15th century, after a siege. It was rebuilt by the Medici and Hapsburg-Lorraine families in the 17th and 18th centuries and rapidly regained its former fame. To mention but a few of the many illustrious personages who took the waters in San Giuliano, it might suffice to recall Shelley, Byron, Alfieri, Carlo Alberto of Savoy, the English and Danish Royal Families, Murat. The waters of San Giuliano are sulphate-alcaline (41°C) and are beneficial to the bone structure and digestive system. The central bathing establishment was built in the 18th century; it opens, on the rear, onto wide, spacious gardens, leading up to the Kaffee-Haus.

2. SAN MINIATO

From Pisa, one takes the state road Nr. 67 along the Arno valley, in the direction of Florence. There is a long series of towns one encounters in these lower stretches of the Valdarno, which are of a decidedly industrial nature: **Cascina**, that produces furniture; **Pontedera**, an important metal-working centre; **Ponsacco**, another furniture manufacturing locality; **Montopoli** with its textile mills. Then one comes to San Miniato situated along the crests of three hills, overlooking the valley.

SAN MINIATO

SAN MINIATO – The history of this small, but extremely lively village is a compendium of everything most typically Medieval: the town's factions fought each other bitterly, it fell under the sway of one overlord after another, it ranged itself staunchly on the Ghibelline side and expressed its deeply felt religious vocation.

The town was an off-shoot of a town in the valley, at the feet of the three hills: San Genesio. In the course of about two hundred years, the new town usurped the position of the old one, to the extent that the latter was destroyed. Even then (12th century) San Miniato was so dear to the Holy Roman Empire that it was called San Miniato al Tedesco (German) and was one of the chief philo-imperial bases in the area. In 1178, Frederick Redbeard himself stayed there. Matilda of Canossa was born there, as well as the painter Ludovico Cardi, known as Cigoli. It contains many interesting buildings, such as **San Domenico**, which possesses a monumental sepulchre by Rossellino in its Samminiati chapel, as well as works by Mariotto di Nardo, by Masolino's Workshop and Galileo Chini. The Cathedral opens onto a grassy terrace looking out over the valley below; abutting onto the terrace one finds the Palace of the Emperor's Representatives **Palazzo dei Vicari dell'Imperatore** (13th century) and the **Cathedral**; the church has a Roman façade and a massive bell-tower called "Matilda's Tower"; at the top of the hill one can see the tower in which Pier delle Vigne was injustly imprisoned and blinded (the fate of this luckless minister of Frederick II was sung by Dante in his *Divine Comedy*). **San Francesco**, a 13th century church, that was restructured in the 15th, has a lovely late-Romanesque façade.

San Giuliano Terme - The entrance to the Baths.

San Miniato - The massive Cathedral Bell Tower, known as «Matilda Tower».

Calci - The imposing façade of the Chartreuse. Below: **San Miniato** - View.

3. VOLTERRA

From Pisa one proceeds along state road Nr. 67 until one gets to Pontedera, then one shears off in the direction of Ponsacco and one follows road Nr. 439 along the valley of the Era, a tributary of the Arno, aiming south. Shortly after Ponsacco, one comes to **Camugliano**, with its 16th century four-towered *Medici Villa*. From Capannoli, a side-road leads to **Casciana Terme**, an ancient watering place, surrounded by softly rolling hills; in Casciana Alta, inside the church of **San Niccolò**, one can admire a lovely panel painted by Lippo Memmi. Proceeding along the course of the Era, through carefully cultivated farmlands, one soon comes within sight of Volterra, at the top of its fortified hill.

VOLTERRA – A veritable compendium of Tuscan history, from the times of the Etruscans to the Middle Ages. Volterra preserves the austere, somewhat mysterious attraction of its origins, both as regards the lay-out of the town, as well as from the point of view of its richly varied art-treasures. Its most renowned and flourishing activity is the production of alabaster artifacts.

It was a prosperous town as far back in time as the Iron Age, when it first emerged as one of the most important Etruscan centres – its name then was *Velathri* – and ruled over extensive dominions from its powerfully fortified hilltop. In the 3rd century B.C., it had already fallen under the sway of Rome and its population numbered some 25,000 inhabitants, placing it among the most densely populated metropolis' of the times. During the 16th century Volterra was included in the Grand Duchy of Tuscany; the peaceful era that ensued unfortunately witnessed a tragic succession of plague and malaria epidemics. The visit of the town can commence from the Medieval walls, which are not as extensive as the former Etruscan fortifications, but include certain sections of them, such as the Gate at the Arch (**Porta all'Arco**) which bears three Etruscan heads which were inserted into the arch during the Roman era. The centre of the town is the **Piazza dei Priori**, surrounded by severe Medieval buildings, such as the **Palazzo dei Priori** which was, in all likelihood, the earliest public administration building in Tuscany (founded in 1208) and was certainly the model many other such buildings were based on: its stone façade is pierced by twin-mullioned windows and bears a series of armorial crests all over the lower section; its bell tower is battlemented; inside, one not only finds the municipal offices, but also, in the great Council Chamber, a 14th century *Annunciation*. Behind the palace, that was the headquarters of the civic administrators, one finds the centre of the religious power wielders: Piazza San Giovanni with the Cathedral and Baptistery. The **Cathedral** (12th century) has a simple Romanesque façade; the 16th century interior contains a 13th century *pulpit*, and a wooden *Deposition* of the same period inside one of the chapels leading off the right transept, a beautiful *shrine* by Mino da Fiesole (1471) on the main altar and a *Procession of the Magi* by Benozzo Gozzoli in the chapel of the Addolorata (Sorrowful Madonna). The **Baptistery** is a 12th century Romanesque building, possessing a baptismal font by Sansovino (1502) as well as an altar by Mino da Fiesole. Next to the Cathedral is the Diocesan Museum of Religious Art (**Museo diocesano di arte sacra**). The most evocative part of the Medieval section of the town is probably the *Quadrivio dei Buomparenti*, the crossing of Via Roma with Via Ricciarelli, which is where the tower-mansion of the Buomparenti stands. In neighbouring Via dei Sarti, inside **Palazzo Solaini**, one finds the Volterra Picture Gallery (**Pinacoteca**), containing paintings by Luca Signorelli, Domenico Ghirlandaio, Rosso Fiorentino and Neri di Bicci. Via Ricciarelli leads to the church of **San Francesco**, where one can admire the frescoed early 15th century cycle of the *Stories of the Cross* – in the chapel of the Croce di Giorno (Cross of the Day). On the other side of the town, beneath the **Fortress** (now used as a prison) overlooking Volterra, one finds the Guarnacci Etruscan Museum (**Museo Etrusco Guarnacci**). It is one of the best-endowed Etruscan collections in Tuscany and contains over 600 cinerary urns (the alabaster ones are particularly fine), as well as an impressive collection of bronze statuettes (including the famous *Evening Shadow*), Roman artifacts, ivories, coins and weapons. Leaving Volterra via the San Francesco Gate one can reach the **Balze** (Cliffs), which are an impressive series of eroded tufa cliffs which, over the centuries have even affected the structure of the town, devouring Etruscan Necropoli, churches, monasteries and dwellings; nearby is an 11th century Camaldolese Abbey, with a façade by Ammannati, that has been abandoned because of its damaged condition and has now fallen into total disrepair thanks to the erosion phenomenon.

Volterra - Piazza dei Priori.

Volterra - Palazzo dei Priori with its distinctive looking tower; below: the park of the Guarnacci Museum.

Volterra - The Fortress, at present used as a prison; below: the Etrusco-Roman Gate at the Arch.

LIVORNO (LEGHORN)

The Canal of the New Fortress.

An industrial centre, but above all one of the main seaports in Italy and one of the most important container-handling ports in the Mediterranean. The industrial growth of the town is closely linked to the fortunes of the harbour and one of the most developed sectors is its petrol refining plant. Tourism and its consequences have chiefly affected a number of locations in the environs of Livorno. The port is also the pivot around which the history of the town revolves: at first it was a harbour of subordinate status in comparision with nearby Pisa; its fortunes prospered in the 14th century, first thanks to its new Genoese overlords, then due to the protection of the Florentines. It was chiefly in the 16th century, under Cosimo I, that Livorno became the "Port of the Medici family". Thanks to a special covenant (it was a free port), by the end of the century its population had doubled, due to the advent of a considerable number of immigrants of the most varied provenance (many of them having come to Livorno to escape from persecution caused by their religion or race). The fortunes of the town continued to prosper under the rule of the Hapsburg-Lorraine family and Leghorn even enjoyed a brief spell during which it became a 19th century seaside resort. It was severely damaged during World War II. Via Grande, with its shops under the porticos, is the main street, leading to the *Cathedral*, a modern edifice, and on the sea-front, to the Monument to the Four Moors (*Monumento ai Quattro Mori*), a 17th century group by Tacca and Giovanni Bandini (who cast the figure of Ferdinando I): the moors represent four Barbary pirates in chains. The **Medici Port** entrance is just opposite the Monument to the Four Moors. Its fortifications were mostly commenced in the 16th century, except for the 15th century eight-sided *Marzocco Tower*, built by the Florentines in 1439 and the Lantern Tower (*Torre del Fanale*), a recent reconstruction of a 14th century tower, beneath which, in the 16th century a lazaret had been built. To the right, one can see the massive **Fortezza Vecchia** (Old Fortress), by Antonio da Sangallo the Younger (1534). On the southern side of the town, overlooking Piazza Mascagni, with its lovely view, is the **Aquarium**. In Piazza Matteotti, in the Public Park, is the **Giovanni Fattori Civic Museum**, containing a considerable collection of this master's works as well as numerous paintings by other artists belonging to the Macchiaioli movement.

The D'Azeglio Piers; below: the sea-side esplanade.

THE ENVIRONS OF LIVORNO

SANCTUARY OF MONTENERO – Famous and much visited, this sanctuary is situated on the hill of Montenero south of Leghorn (a cable-car leads up to it as well).

Founded in the 14th and enlarged over the following centuries (at the end of the 18th century, it was handed over to the Vallombrosan Order), it was constructed to enshrine an icon of Our Lady, that had arrived miraculously, according to the legend, from Greece. A flight of steps leads up to a panoramic terrace, that enjoys a magnificent view over Leghorn and the sea, and is enclosed on the right, by a loggia containing the tombs of illustrious Leghorn citizens. The Baroque church is preceded by a double-pillared portico. Inside, above the main altar, inlaid with semi-precious stones, is the miraculous effigy of the *Madonna and Child*, attributed to the 14th century painter Jacopo di Michele, known also as Gera. See also the enormous collection of ex-voto offerings (chiefly left by sailors), in the sacristy and adjacent corridors.

Monument to Ferdinand I, by Giovanni Bandini; the figures of the Four Moors, after whom the monument is named, were cast by Pietro Tacca; the Old Fortress, by Antonio da Sangallo the Younger. Below: **Montenero** - The Sanctuary at the top of a hill just outside Leghorn.

THE PROVINCE OF LIVORNO

1. The coast south of Livorno: Cecina, Populonia, Piombino —
2. Elba and Capraia.

1. THE COAST SOUTH OF LIVORNO: CECINA, POPULONIA, PIOMBINO

South of Livorno, one can drive down the Via Aurelia along the coast: the landscape is extremely varied, ranging from wide, sandy beaches and rocky coves, from sea-side resorts to large industrial centres, from shady pine groves to carefully tilled farmlands. Just outside Leghorn, one encounters a lovely bay, surrounded by rocky cliffs, called **Calafuria**. Further down the coast, one passes through a number of elegant little holiday resorts, such as **Quercianella**, **Castiglioncello** and, beyond the industrial district of **Rosignano**, **Vada**. Continuing onwards, one reaches **Cecina**, an animated agricultural centre and market town on the banks of the river Cecina. It was founded fairly recently after the successful land reclamation campaign at the beginning of the last century had been concluded. It possesses an interesting **Antiquarium**, which contains the fascinating archaeological finds that have been unearthed all around. Its coastal off-shoot is **Marina di Cecina**, a busy and much frequented seaside resort. Further on, one finds **Bibbona**, with its *Medici Fort*, **Bolgheri** with its Carducci memories (the famous cypresses and the *chapel of San Guido*), **Castagneto**, **Donoratico**, and then **San Vincenzo** and **Populonia**.

POPULONIA

POPULONIA – A little Medieval village perched on the Piombino promontory looking out over the small, but picturesque bay of the gulf of Baratti. It was founded by the Etruscans and was subsequently conquered by the Romans. Ancient Pupluna (the name can only be found on 4th/3rd century B.C. coins) flourished as one of the main ports of the region and as important iron smelting centre — the iron was mined on the nearby island of Elba.

The crest of the hill on which Populonia sits today was the acropolis of the ancient town, protected by its walls, considerable remains of which are still extant; the industrial and naval sections of the town were spread out over the lower slopes of the hill and sea-front. During the Middle Ages, invasions and pillaging troops caused the town's decline and it only regained stature, when it was reconstructed in the 14th century by the Sienese. All around the gulf of Baratti lies the Etruscan **necropolis** that was unearthed at the beginning of the century, after having been concealed for centuries under the smelting works rubble that had been unloaded and strewn all along the coast. The 7th to 2nd century tombs differ as regards type, according to the period in which they were made, the most ancient being the trench type, followed by the chamber type, followed in a more recent era by tumulus type tombs with pseudo-dome roofs, followed later still by shrine-type or chest type tombs (the most renowned being the Flabella Tomb, the Chariots tomb, the Attic Vases Tomb, the Biers Tomb and the Shrine Tomb). The most remarkable archaeological finds from the necropolis are preserved in the Archaeological Museum in Florence, but the material in the small local museum is interesting too.

Beyond the promontory on which Populonia is situated, one enters Piombino.

PIOMBINO

PIOMBINO – Situated on the southern side of the promontory, opposite the island of Elba, it is the nearest ferry harbour on the mainland, for anyone wishing to get to the island; metal-working industries and steel-foundries constitute the town's most flourishing activity and comprise the largest plants of their kind in Tuscany.

It used to be a Roman town, known as Porto Falesia; in the 12th and 13th centuries it was a vital Pisan bridge-head, and later became part of the territories of the Appiani family, lords of Pianosa, Elba and Montecristo. In the 19th century, under Napoleon, it was first annexed by the French Empire and thereafter granted to Elisa Bonaparte Baciocchi, sister to Napoleon and Princess of Lucca. The Congress of Vienna (1815) bound its destinies to those of the Grand Duchy of Tuscany, placing it under the latter's sway. The town possesses interesting Medieval and Renaissance buildings (the old **fortifications**, the **Communal Palace**, the church of **Sant'Antimo**), a magnificent view over the Channel of Piombino and the Tuscan Archipelago can be enjoyed from Piazza Bovio, which is rather like a great terrace overlooking the sea.

Calafuria - The Castle.

Castiglioncello - The Pasquini Castle.
Piombino - The Terrace.

Populonia - The Etruscan Necropolis; below, right: a stretch of coastline south of Leghorn.

Populonia - Above: The Tomb of the Bronze Statuette; below: tumulus-tomb.

ISLAND OF ELBA

ISLAND OF ELBA – It is the largest island in the Tuscan Archipelago. There are a lot of iron-ore mines on Elba, but it is chiefly renowned for its beauty and is one of the main holiday resorts in Tuscany. All the towns and villages on the island are connected to each other by excellent roads that offer one magnificent views.

All along the jagged, rocky, high-cliffed coastline of Elba one finds a multitude of enchanting little inlets and beaches. The water is clear, bright blue and green; the island is full of hills and mountains (the highest one is the granite peak of Monte Capanne), covered with the thickety scrub of the Mediterranean; higher up, one wanders through woods of deciduous trees; the climate is mild and the cultivated land luxuriant and fruitful (a number of delicious wines are produced on the island, among which the famous Aleatico); daily ferryboats ply to and from between the island and Piombino and Leghorn on the mainland. The most important towns on the island are Portoferraio (the capital of the island), Porto Azzurro (erstwhile Portolongone), Rio nell'Elba, Rio Marina on the east coast; Capoliveri to the north-west; and Campo nell'Elba to the south. Inhabited in the remotest past by the Ilvates, a Ligurian tribe, who gave the ancient name of Ilva (whence Elba) to the island, it became part of the Etruscan territories, who ably exploited its mineral resources, much as their successors, the Romans did; the latter also used the island as a vital naval base. In the Middle Ages, Elba belonged to Pisa and suffered frequent inroads from the Genoese as well as marauding attacks from the Saracens. After he was defeated, Napoleon Bonaparte was sent to Elba, in exile, in May 1814 and managed to escape from the island the February of the following year — he had been granted the sovereignity of the island. After Napoleon's escape, it was incorporated in the territories of the Tuscan Grand Duchy, the destinies of which it thereafter followed. **Portoferraio**, the main town and harbour of the island, derives its name from the iron-ore mines all around it. The fortresses of the Falcon and the Star (*Falcone* and *Stella*) — lovely views over the town and bay — are vivid examples of the fortifications Cosimo I had built on the island against the Turkish peril. The Napoleonic era gave Elba the **House of Napoleon**, which was the Emperor's residence, in which he lived with his court (relics, pictures and a well-stocked library), as well as **Villa San Martino** (six kms from Portoferraio, which was the Emperor's summer residence. The Forese Gallery (**Pinacoteca Foresiana**) is part of the complex and contains a number of 16th and 17th century works, but is chiefly full of 19th century paintings (by Fattori, Signorini, Bezzuoli, Canova and Corcos). Not far from the town, in a locality known as Le Grotte, one can moreover visit the remains of a Roman villa of the Imperial era with a large pool (interesting water-heating system still visible), as well as other appurtenances. Not far from Campo dell'Elba is **Marina di Campo**, overlooking its bay, with one of the finest beaches on the island. **Marciana**, a busy little wine-producing village, contains the remains of an old castle that belonged to the Appiani family and an **Antiquarium** with archaeological material, unearthed locally. Lower down, on the sea-front is **Marciana Marina** with its typical little harbour. **Capoliveri**, in a fine position with a lovely view, is a typical little mining town. **Porto Azzurro** is a picturesque little village with a charming pleasure-craft harbour. The 17th century **fortress of Portolongone** (used today as a prison), that was commissioned by Philip III of Spain, commands the view from above the harbour. Lastly, **Rio nell'Elba** and **Rio Marina**, surrounded by russety ferrous hills (see the little **Mineralogical Museum** and, after obtaining authorisation, the mines), are the most important mining centres on the island.

CAPRAIA

CAPRAIA – The island is connected with Leghorn, by means of a ferry service (there are more runs in summer-time, as well as a ferry service connecting Capraia to Portoferraio).

The island towers above the sea with its reddish cliffs, nearer Corsica than Italy, about an hour's distance from the coast. Totally devoid of any tourist attractions, it is the ideal spot for lovers of solitude and sea-bathing. Archaeologists have dug-up ancient Neolithic sites on Capraia; there are also a few Etruscan ones as well as a greater number of Roman locations. After the unification of Italy, Capraia became a penal colony (which was only closed in 1986). A little harbour, surrounded by a few houses, 800 ms. of asphalted road leading up to the village and to the Fortress of St. George (**Forte di San Giorgio**), and a couple of churches are the only man-made things on the island (as well, of course, as the prison).

Island of Elba - View of Portoferraio; below: view of Porto Azzurro.

Island of Capraia - Fort of St. George (Forte San Giorgio).

Island of Elba - View. Below: **Island of Capraia** - The little harbour.

GROSSETO

Grosseto started existing in the 10th century, when the inhabitants of nearby Roselle, together with all their activities moved to the new site after their native town had been razed to the ground by the Saracens. A Free Commune in the 12th century, it was conquered by the Sienese and finally, in the 16th century, it was incorporated by the Medici Grand Duchy. The most important town in the Maremma, endemic malaria caused its fortunes to decline and its population to dwindle until the 18th/19th centuries, when land reclamation campaigns improved the situation. The diminutive historical centre of the town is surrounded by six-sided fortified ramparts (built by order of the Medici) and comprises the main monuments.

CATHEDRAL – Built during the 13th/14th centuries, it was restructured many times in successive centuries. The façade is modern. Inside, one finds a *baptismal font* as well as a 15th century reredos, and a fine panel painted by Matteo di Giovanni depicting the *Assumption*. A building to the left of the Cathedral contains the **Diocesan Museum**, where one can admire a collection of illuminated manuscript codexes, paintings by Sassetta and other Sienese masters.

SAN FRANCESCO – A 13th century Gothic church, containing 14th century frescoes and a fine *Crucifix* attributed to Duccio di Buoninsegna.

ARCHAEOLOGICAL MUSEUM – A rich collection of archaeological finds unearthed all over the province of Grosseto, from Vetulonia to Roselle to Sovana: Villanovian ossuaries, Italic ceramics, coins, Etruscan urns and bronze statuettes, Roman sculpture.

The Romanesque apse of the church of San Pietro.

ARCHAEOLOGICAL MUSEUM - A room; below: the head and torso of a stone statue, from the Tumulus of Pietrera, in Vetulonia, now in the museum.

THE ENVIRONS OF GROSSETO

1. ROSELLE

The ruins of Roselle are not far from Grosseto, in the direction of Siena.

ROSELLE – Situated a few kilometres away from Grosseto, it boasts important archaeological finds that are still being excavated. The town used to be one of the most important centres in Northern Etruria; it belonged to the powerful confederation of twelve Etruscan cities, known as the Dodecapolis.

Mentioned in the works of Dionysius of Halicarnassus and Livy, according to whom Roselle was conquered by the Romans in 294 B.C. In the 5th century, it was an important Bishopric, the seat of which was transferred to Grosseto in 1138, by Pope Innocent III. The 3.2 Km. long fortifications are still extant, together with what is left of six city gates. The most ancient remains are on the northern and eastern sides (4th century B.C.), whereas the south-eastern side reveals later additions (2nd century B.C.). Inside the walls, on the northern side, there are two Etruscan dwellings, respectively of the 7th and 6th century B.C., the former in unbaked bricks, the other in stone with portions of plaster still present. Also at the northern end of the town, at the top of a slight rise, one can admire the remains of an amphitheatre of the Augustan era; at the foot of the hillock, one finds the ruins of the Imperial Forum, of which one can distinguish a street along which rises a basilica built in the times of Augustus, revealing additions made in successive periods. South west of the Forum, there is another basilica dedicated to Divo Augusto (the divine Augustus), from which 14 statues have been removed and taken to the Archaeological Museum of Grosseto. East of the Forum are the ruins of an end of the 1st century construction, known as the "villa", that was in likelihood the Baths, which was partially transformed, during the late Imperial era, into a Christian basilica.

Grosseto - Piazza del Duomo (Cathedral square). Below: **Roselle** - The remains of the so-called «Villa» a Roman 1st century B.C. building that was probably the Baths.

THE PROVINCE OF GROSSETO

1. Vetulonia, Massa Marittima — 2. The Wildlife Reserve of the Uccellina — 3. Orbetello, Argentario, Ansedonia — 4. Islands of Giglio and Giannutri; 5. Saturnia, Sovana, Sorano, Pitigliano, Santa Fiora.

1. VETULONIA, MASSA MARITTIMA

One leaves Grosseto bearing northwards along the Aurelia, until Braccagni; then right, along a side-road to **Montepescali**, a Medieval village that still possesses most of the impressive fortifications it was endowed with by the Sienese in the 16th century; see also the fine Romanesque-Gothic church of **San Lorenzo**, and the even more ancient church of **San Niccolò**, near the (torre del Cassero) Keep tower, with 14th century frescoes. Proceeding along the Aurelia until Grilli, one takes a lovely twisting road up to Vetulonia.

VETULONIA – A Medieval looking village, situated on top of the acropolis of what used to be an important Etruscan metropolis, that belonged to the league of twelve towns (Dodecapolis) built on the shores of Lake Prile (that no longer exists today).

It was only at the end of the 19th century that the village of Poggio Colonna was identified as having being built on the site of ancient Vetluna, whereupon it was given its present name to celebrate the important discovery. The archaeological finds unearthed have revealed that the town flourished most splendidly in the 7th century and survived — in somewhat declining circumstances — until the 2nd century A.D., when it was destroyed and forgotten. Only the so-called **Arce Walls** survive to reminds us of what the (originally 5 Km.- long) walls of the town used to look like: it is a short section of Etruscan wall between two Medieval watch-towers, whereas the other finds dug-up all over the area have been chronologically arranged in the **Antiquarium** (but the most important items have been taken to the Archaeological Museum in Florence). The most interesting part of the finds however is the vast necropolis area just outside the town: Poggio alla Guardia, Poggio alle Birbe and Poggio al Bello to the east; Colle Baroncio, Poggio Valli and Dupiane to the west. The most ancient tombs (10th-7th centuries) are well-shaped (a pozzo), and the furnishings for the dead, inside, are sparse, whereas after the middle of the 8th century, one finds circular tombs, full of splendid furnishings and in even more recent centuries (7th-6th), the Etruscans of Vetulonia started using the tumulus type tombs, where items of enormous interest have been found. Two of the latter are still visible: the **Tumulus of Pietrera** and the Tumulus of the little Devil Nr. 2 (**tumulo del Diavolino**).

Returning to the Aurelia, one continues along it until Gavorrano station, where one turns off right in the direction of Massa.

MASSA MARITTIMA – A town of great artistic interest, possessing a pronounced Medieval flavour. The town is divided into two sections: the lower old town, with the more ancient monuments and the new town, higher up. All around there are numerous mineral deposits.

Constructed upon the probable site of an earlier Etruscan settlement, Massa was an important Bishop's Seat as from the 9th century; thanks to the nearby copper and silver mines, it soon became a prosperous and powerful Free Commune (the oldest known code of mining legislation was compiled in Massa in 1310); it was however unable to withstand the Sienese armies and in 1335 was definitely absorbed into the Sienese territories; in the 16th century, it became part of the Grand Duchy of Tuscany. The irregular shaped Piazza Garibaldi, surrounded by remarkably beautiful buildings, is the heart of the old town. The **Praetorian Palace** (founded around 1230), with its façade covered with the armorial bearings of the Podestàs who resided in it (15th-17th centuries), and pierced by two orders of twin-mullioned windows, encloses the **Archaeological Museum**, containing interesting Etruscan finds, as well as the Civic Picture Gallery (*Pinacoteca Civica*), where one can admire a lovely *Madonna and Child enthroned*, by Ambrogio Lorenzetti. The massive **Communal Palace**, a battlemented building with three orders of twin-mullioned windows was formed by incorporating several 13th/14th century tower-

Vetulonia - The so-called «Mura dell'Arce».

Massa Marittima - The Cathedral; below: the Tomb of St. Cerbone (1324), beneath the Cathedral.

Vetulonia - The Tomb of the Belvedere.

Vetulonia - The parish church with its massive bell tower. Below: **Massa Marittima** - The entrance of the Fortress of the Sienese.

Massa Marittima - The Communal Palace; below: the Palace of «Abbondanza» (1265), where the Sienese Administration housed the grain deposit (on the upper storey), when they were running the town.

mansions into a single building. The **Cathedral**, a Romanesque-Gothic jewel, is an imposing Pisan-type construction placed at the top of a stage-like ramp of steps; it was founded around the beginning of the 13th century and completed about one hundred years later. The blind-arcaded façade is set unusually obliquely to the square and creates an accentuated perspective fugue, inasmuch as the distance between the semicolumns on the right is less than that on the left; the fine main entrance is carved in relief with *Episodes from the life of St. Cerbone*, the saint to whom the church is dedicated. The upper portion of the façade has two superimposed loggias (the lower arcade is blind and the central portion is occupied by a great rose-window; the upper arcade, by a pupil of Giovanni Pisano, is interrupted in the centre by a great four-mullioned window). The majestic belltower stands to the left of the Cathedral. The interior is divided into a nave and two side-aisles and contains a great *baptismal font* (1267) by Giroldo da Como, a 13th century *Crucifix*, as well as the *Madonna of Mercy*, attributed to Duccio; in the chambers beneath the church is the *sepulchre of St. Cerbone*, sculpted in 1324. The new town surrounds the **Fortress of the Sienese**, that was built after Siena managed to gain control of Massa. The church of **Sant'Agostino** (end 13th-beginning 14th cents.) is very fine, with an imposing portal and an aisle-less interior with a poligonal apse.

From Massa, proceeding along state road Nr. 73 towards the sea, one gets to **Follonica**, with its fine beaches sheltered by mile-long pine-groves. The town enjoyed its greatest industrial expansion during the last century, when the surrounding countryside was finally freed of malaria and the traditional foundries and smelting activities of the area were given a new lease of life thanks to the Grand Duke's policy of encouraging local activities. The church of *San Leopoldo* is in fact dedicated to the Saint after whom the Grand Duke of the time was christened. Continuing southwards along the coast road, one encounters a succession of enchanting views of the surrounding countyside, which is a blend of Mediterranean scrub, pine woods and rocky outcrops; one arrives finally at **Punta Ala**, situated at the tip of the point that encloses the bay of Follonica. The place has just recently been "developed" and now boasts a little harbour, hotels, sport facilities, etc. Further south, towards Marina di Grosseto, one finds **Castiglione della Pescaia**. A well-known and fully equipped seaside resort, surrounded by dense pine woods, holiday residences and a large number of camp-sites, it is also an important fishing port. The village is divided into two sections: a modern, lower section and a Medieval (*Castiglione Castello*), fortified part, crowded around a frowning Aragonese Fortress (*Rocca*) dating back to the 14th/15th century.

2. The National Reserve of the Uccellina

THE UCCELLINA – A magnificent wildlife reserve, it comprises a short stretch of the Grosseto coastline, between Marina di Alberese and Talamone, which has been spared the disastrous transformations inflicted on the rest of the Tuscan sea-board, thanks to the foundation of this wildlife reserve park, in the Maremma, in 1975.

One is allowed to visit the park on public holidays, Saturdays and Wednesdays, from 9 a.m. until one hour before sunset: one must keep to the paths traced by the management and it is obviously forbidden to cause any damage to flora and fauna. The starting-out point is in Alberese. A mini-bus drives one to a certain point, then one gets out and continues on foot. There are four basic itineraries: the San Rabano path, the Cala di Forno track, the Towers itinerary and the Cave path, all easy to follow and full of delightful surprises. **San Rabano** used to be a Benedictine monastery, founded around the 11th century and demolished in the 15th century by order of the Sienese: the remains of the Romanesque church with a beautiful main entrance, an octagonal dome and bell tower are still extant. **Cala di Forno** is a lovely bay, a natural harbour, exploited in the past by wood and coal transport vessels. The place is linked to the legend of the "Fair Marsilia" (her real name was Margherita), who was the only survivor of the Sienese Marsili family, who were the lords of the area and were massacred by invading pirates. The beautiful maiden was born off to the harem of Suleiman the Great, whose legitimate and blissful bride she became, in due course, (to the extent that she refused to return to her native land when she was offered the opportunity). Every hill or outcrop in the Uccellina is crowned by a tower: they are the watch towers, some of them Medieval, all of which were included in the powerful defensive system of the State of the "Presidi" organised by Philip II in the 16th century (Presidi means fortified garrisons). The caves, on the other hand are to be found along the rocky sides of the Uccellina mountains. The largest are to be found to the north of the plain of Castelmarino.

Punta Ala - The harbour.

Castiglione della Pescaia - View; below: the modern part of the village, dominated by the Aragonese Fort.

The Wildlife Reserve of the Uccellina - Overall view. Below, right: **Orbetello** - The Spanish Gate.

Orbetello - The Municipal Palace; below: the Lagoon at sunset.

3. ORBETELLO, ARGENTARIO, ANSEDONIA

After the Uccellina one continues southwards along the Aurelia until Orbetello Scalo, from where a road branches-off towards the promontory of the Argentario, traversing the lagoon that divides it from the coast by means of the central tongue of land of the three (they are known as "tomboli"), that link the Argentario to the mainland. Half-way across is Orbetello.

ORBETELLO – An active fishing and industrial centre, that grew up on the narrow strip of land that divides the lagoon of Orbetello in half; it is joined to Monte Argentario by means of an artificial dike.

It was probably founded way back, in the 7th century B.C. (large portions of the town walls date back to the ancient 4th century fortifications). It was the domain of various overlords, until the Orsini family gained possession of it in the 14th century and held it for about one hundred years; then the Sienese held it for another century until the Spaniards managed to possess themselves of it, transforming it into the capital of their bristling Garrison State (Stato dei Presidi), which also included Porto Ercole, Porto Santo Stefano, together with Monte Argentario, Talamone and Porto Azzurro. The town still bears evident traces of the Spanish domination, in the powerful fortifications erected on the landward side between the 16th and 17th centuries as well as in Fort Guzman, which is the seat of the Communal Etrusco-Roman Museum (**Museo Comunale Etrusco Romano**) which contains an interesting collection of locally excavated archaeological material. The **Cathedral** was founded in the 14th century, and still preserves its original façade, with a finely sculpted main portal, as well as a lovely pre-Romanesque altar-front inside, although it was restructured in the 17th century.

ARGENTARIO – Monte Argentario's main attraction is the beauty of its coast-line, mostly high and rocky, the trasparency of its waters, and the sparkling variety of greens in its magnificent Mediterranean scrub, which is continually being threatened by savage fires and senseless residential developments.

One of the most important centres on the promontory, **Porto Ercole**, opens onto a little bay on the eastern side. In 1610, Michelangelo Merisi, known as Caravaggio, died there of malaria — he had been one of the greatest Italian Baroque masters. The severe, frowning shapes of Forte Stella, Forte Filippo as well as the other fortresses, crowning every hilltop around the harbour, are vivid reminders of the Spanish domination, during which Porto Ercole was part of the Garrison State (Stato dei Presidi). **Palazzo Consani** (16th century) is another reminder of the Spanish occupation, as it was the Governor's residence. See also (after asking for permission) the fascinating private gardens of **Villa Corsini**, which contain a collection of rare tropical plants. **Porto Santo Stefano**, on the north-western side of the promontory, is a fishing harbour and well-known sea-bathing resort, housing the Municipal Offices of Monte Argentario. The town was founded by Elban and Ligurian fishermen between the 15th and 16th centuries and became a thriving trading harbour during the Spanish domination (16th-17th centuries); most of Porto Santo Stefano has been built fairly recently, as it was considerably damaged during the last war. The old part is still attractive, with the severe bulk of the 17th century Spanish Fortress (Rocca) towering above the old buildings.

Returning to the Aurelia, one proceeds to Ansedonia, situated at the mainland end of the tombolo di Feniglia (the third strip that links the Argentario to the mainland).

ANSEDONIA – The archaeological site with the ruins of the ancient city of Cosa, believed to have been an important 3rd century B.C. Roman colony, is spread all over the crest of the promontory of Ansedonia, enjoying a magnificent view over the sea.

One enters the ancient city via the **Roman Gate**, which is the one that has survived best of the three gates belonging to the imposing fortifications, and encounters the network of roads laid out at right angles to each other in characteristic Roman geometrical fashion, leading up to the fortified **Acropolis**. Various remains of the **Forum** are still extant, revealing that it used to possess a basilica, two temples, the law-courts (curia) and a market. One can also distinguish the **Capitol** divided into three large halls. At the foot of the promontory, there used to be the ancient port of Cosa, protected from an excessive influx of silt (which in due course was exactly what led to the decline of the port), by the so-called **Tagliata etrusca** (Etruscan Cutting), a magnif-

Monte Argentario - A view of the coastline.

Ansedonia - Above and below: the remains of the ancient Roman town.

Porto Ercole - The small bay and harbour. Below: **Porto Santo Stefano** - View.

icent engineering feat carried out by Roman hydraulic experts, that enabled water to flow in and out in the same way in which it flowed through the **Spacco della Regina** (Cleft of the Queen), a natural cleft, slightly altered by man that forms a very impressive passage through the rocks. Remains of the jetties of the Roman harbour are visible just below the surface of the water, out in the bay, whereas remains of a Roman villa and storehouses can be seen near the **Torre della Tagliata** (Tower of the Cutting). After the fortunes of Cosa declined (5th century A.D.), it was succeeded by Ansedonia, founded a little later, not far from the ruins of the old town around the middle of the 14th century. It survived for a few centuries in varying circumstances, and was finally destroyed by Siena. The Ansedonia of today bears the name of the Medieval town and is a very popular seaside resort.

4. THE ISLANDS OF GIGLIO AND GIANNUTRI

Ferryboats to the two small islands of the Tuscan Archipelago leave from Porto Santo Stefano, on the Argentario, and dock-in at Giglio Porto, departing thence, during the holiday season, to Giannutri.

THE ISLAND OF GIGLIO – It has become a well-known holiday resort and is the second largest island in the Tuscan Archipelago, both as regards surface and population. The shape of the isle is elliptical and it is extremely hilly (the highest peak is Poggio della Pagana (498 ms), but intensely cultivated and possessing a widely varied fauna. The island lies opposite the Argentario and contains the villages of Giglio Porto, Giglio Castello and Campese.

Its coasts are mostly granite cliffs, with very few beaches (Campese beach is lovely, though). It was already inhabited in pre-historic times, then it was colonised by the Etruscans and later on, in Roman times, became the private estate of the Domitian Aenobarbus family, who owned the villa, one can see the remains of, near the port. It was attacked several times by the pirates and towards the middle of the 16th century, it became part of the Grand Duchy of Tuscany, following the latter's destinies. Giglio Castello, perched at the top of a hill in the centre of the island, surrounded by its Medieval walls and watched over by its 14th century Fortress (Rocca), is most picturesque.

THE ISLAND OF GIANNUTRI – It is a little private island shaped like a sickle and situated south-east of Giglio.

The surface of the island is rugged (Capel Rosso is the highest spot, near the southern point of the island) and its steep, rocky coast-line is covered with lush Mediterranean scrub, populated by a wide variety of animals. It was deserted for a long time, until 1861, when a lighthouse was built on the island. Before that it had belonged to the Grand Duchy of Tuscany: earlier still it had been a pirate haven and during the Middle Ages, Cistercian monks had lived on it. During the Roman era, when it was known as Artemisia, or Dianium, it belonged to the Domitian Aenobarbus family: the evocative remains of a 1st century A.D. Roman villa still bear witness to their ownership.

5. SATURNIA, SOVANA, SORANO, PITIGLIANO, SANTA FIORA

The itinerary winds through the wildest and loneliest part of the Tuscan Maremma, a land full of vineyards and Etruscan remains. From Grosseto, one proceeds towards south-east, along state-road Nr. 322 and after Scansano and Montemerano one takes a side-road leading to **Saturnia**, a well-known hot springs watering place (37.5°C.), where the sulphurous waters are beneficial against a host of afflictions. Tradition states it was the most ancient town on the Italic peninsula, founded by the god or mythical king whose name it bears. First an Etruscan and then a Roman possession, it failed to recover its strength after it was ravaged by the Sienese in the 14th century (Siena tried vainly to make it flourish again during the following century); the Sienese built the 15th century fortifications — still extant — which were erected on top of the pre-existing ancient, probably pre-Etruscan walls). Not far off is an interesting **necropolis** where one can see simple travertine individual tombs. Proceeding along the same road, one reaches Sovana.

SOVANA – A fascinating little town, plunged in the silence of its medieval lanes.

Of ancient origins, it was an Etruscan town first, then a Roman one, blossoming into its splendid heyday in the Middle Ages, under the Aldobran-

Island of Giglio - The entrance to the Castle.

Island of Giannutri - Cala Maestra.
Saturnia - The hot sulphureous water springs.

Island of Giglio - One of its lovely inlets. Below, right: **Sovana** - The Ildebranda Tomb.

Sovana - Piazza del Pretorio; below: the interior of the Cathedral.

deschi family. Its decline set in when it was taken over by the Orsini family in the 14th century and continued after it was conquered by the Sienese in the following century. When the Archbishop's Seat was shifted to Pitigliano (1660), while malaria raged unchecked, it did not help much, notwithstanding various measures decided upon by the Gran Ducal government to improve the situation of the town. The famous Pope Gregory VII (1073-1085), the pope who started the terrible investiture quarrel off, was born here. As soon as one enters the little town, one encounters the remains of the ancient castle of the Aldobrandeschi. Proceeding along the main street of the village, between little Medieval houses, one reaches Piazza del Pretorio, where one finds the 13th century **Praetorian Palace**, which was restructured in the 15th century and on successive occasions, the **Bourbon del Monte Palace** (16th century) and the little church of **Santa Maria**, a 12th century Romanesque structure containing a magnificent 8th-9th century ciborium, a unique example of pre-Romanesque Tuscan art. Just outside the village is the **Cathedral**, that was built between the 12th and 14th century; it possesses a dome covered externally by an octagonal drum; the portal is finely carved (on the left flank) and the majestic interior has a central nave separated from the side-aisles by pillars with beautifully sculpted capitals. Not far from Sovana there is an important Etruscan necropolis where most of the tombs are of the the chamber type, dating from the 4th-3rd centuries B.C.

Just beyond Sovana, the road forks, leading (in one direction, towards Sorano, in the other towards Pitigliano).

Sorano - View.

SORANO – A picturesque little village in which nothing seems to have changed since the Middle Ages, built, like Pitigliano on a tufa outcrop overlooking the valley of the Lente.

Founded by the Etruscans, it was part of the Aldobrandeschi domain in the Middle Ages; thereafter it was ruled over by the Orsini and, at the beginning of the 17th century, was incorporated into the Grand Duchy of Tuscany. The **parish church**, restructured in the Neo-classical mode, stands on the main square. By means of a nearby 16th century doorway, one enters a charming courtyard, which is all that is left on the ancient Count's Palace (**Palazzo Comitale**), the erstwhile residence of the lords of the area, before the 15th century fortress of the Orsini family (that overlooks the little town, commanding an extensive view of the surrounding countryside) was built.

PITIGLIANO – Built on top of a massive block of tufa pierced through and through by the tunnels of ancient Etruscan tombs and constructed out of the same material so that it has the spectacular appearance of a vast and powerful sculpture, in which the houses appears to be carved directly into the cliffs they cling to, sheer above the deep ravine below.

Sorano - A picturesque view of the little town; below: Etruscan cliff tombs.

The site seems to have been inhabited since the most ancient times; it belonged to the Etruscans, then it became a Roman town. In the Middle Ages, the Aldobrandeschi family was followed by the Orsini, a powerful family of the Roman aristocracy, under whose sway the town prospered, casting neighbouring Sovana in the shade. Thereafter it became a demesne of the Strozzi family, and later still of the Medici and Hapsburg-Lorraine lines, when it was annexed by the Grand Dukedom of Tuscany. Pitigliano's unique historical centre boasts Renaissance and Late-Renaissance constructions in a purely Medieval setting, such as the imposing, battlemented **Orsini Palace**, that was founded in the 14th century and added-to in later centuries (the 16th century changes were planned by Giuliano da Sangallo); one reaches it by walking along the monumentally imposing aqueduct commissioned by the Orsini family, too, in the 16th century.

From Sorano, a fine road traverses a lonely stretch of countryside, on its way towards the Amiata (see Itinerary 3 of the Province of Siena) and Santa Fiora.

SANTA FIORA – A holiday resort, and onetime demesne of the Aldobrandeschi family, it became part of the Grand Duchy of Tuscany at the end of the 18th century.

The village is divided into two sections: the Castle and the burg. The former, up on the hill-side, surrounds the remains of the **Rocca** (Fortress) of the Aldobrandeschi; the **Palazzo Sforza Cesarini** is of interest, as well as the Romanesque **Parish Church**, which was much restructured during the Renaissance, when the lovely doorway and a number of Della Robbia reliefs were added to the church. Down in the walled burg one can visit the **Fishpool** that was built in the 18th century to capture the river Fiora's spring water.

Pitigliano - Overall view of the town and its fortifications. Below: **Santa Fiora** - The 18th century fish-pool.

SIENA

Legend has it that Siena was founded by Aschius and Senius sons of Remus (founder, along with his brother Romulus, of Rome) on three hillsides. According to another legend, the city was founded by a Gallic tribe, the Senoni — and, in fact, by, the Imperial Age it was a Roman dominion under the name *Sena Julia.* In 1147, a burgeoning center of trade and commerce, it abandoned the feudal form of government, becoming a free commune. This marked the beginning of its period of greatest splendor, but also of greatest torment. Throughout the 12th and 13th centuries bitter power struggles went on both on the inside (among local factions) and on the outside (Ghibelline Siena vs. Guelph Florence). Despite the incessant warring, Siena's great banking and merchant families prospered on Europe-wide trade. The tide turned in the mid-1200s following the Sienese army's defeat of the Florentines at Montaperti, Siena's victory meant a short-lived supremacy of the antipapal forces, while the Pope retaliated not only by excommunicating the whole city, but also by cutting off business relations with the Sienese banks — which worried the populace just as much. Consequently, most of Ghibelline Siena swiftly converted into pro-Pope Guelphs, with the end result that the economy began to prosper once more and peace reigned again in Tuscany. Then in the mid-1300s more troubles arose in the wake of the terrible plague epidemic, the Black Death, which struck in 1348, decimating the population and causing political and economic instabilty. Around the end of the century Siena became a dominion of the Viscontis and then part of the *Signoria* of Pandolfo Petrucci. In 1555, after a seemingly endless siege, it succumbed to Florence, never really regaining its political independence in the centuries that followed. During the Middle Ages, Siena flourished artistically as well as politically. For two centuries (13th and 14th) the Sienese school, represented by Duccio di Buoninsegna, Simone Martini, and the Lorenzetti brothers, rivaled the Florentine masters as the most important in Italy. Two celebrated ecclesiastical figures were natives of Siena. One, a saint (Catherine), lived in the 14th century, while the other, a pope (Pius II) was born a Piccolomini in the early 1400s. Gastronomic treats include coldcuts, olive oil, Chianti wines, and sweets (*panforte* and *ricciarelli* cookies). Twice a year (on July 2 and August 16), the *Palio* is run in Piazza del Campo. More than just a horse race (an unbelievably intense couple of minutes often involving violent falls of horses and/or jockeys), the event requires a whole year of preparation and actually lasts a month (with parties, flag acrobatics, parades, and picturesque customs such as blessing of the horses in church). The rivalry among Siena's 17 *contrade* (districts) dates back to the Middle Ages. Among Siena's numerous cultural organizations, perhaps the most famous is the Accademia Musicale Chigiana, which sponsors summer concerts in the city squares, churches, and theaters.

RECOMMENDED ITINERARIES – A walk through Siena's web of streets is like going back to Middle Ages. To get the most out your tour we propose two itineraries.

1st ITINERARY: Sienese life is centered around **Piazza del Campo** dominated by the town's civic center, **Palazzo Pubblico.** Across the way, take Vicolo di San Pietro which leades to the *Croce del Travaglio,* where many of the main streets intersect (Via di Città, *Via Banchi di Sopra,* and Banchi di Sotto). Proceed along Via Banchi di Sopra (flanked with impressive palaces such as 13th century *Palazzo Tolomei*) to *Piazza Salimbeni,* the site of a Gothic palace, *Palazzo Salimbeni* (while if you take Via della Sapienza on the left you come out at *San Domenico*). Just before reaching Piazza Salimbeni, go right on *Via dei Rossi* to the church of *San Francesco.* Retrace your steps to the Croce del Travaglio, go left along *Via Banchi di Sotto* flanked with important buildings such as the 16th century *Palazzo dell'Università* and **Palazzo Piccolomini.** Passing the 15th century *Logge del Papa,* take Via del Porrione, Via San Martino, and Via dei Servi to the church of **Santa Maria dei Servi.**

Above and below: two moments of the Palio of Siena; opposite and below: map of the town and the colours of the seventeen Contrade of Siena.

AQUILA

BRUCO

CHIOCCIOLA

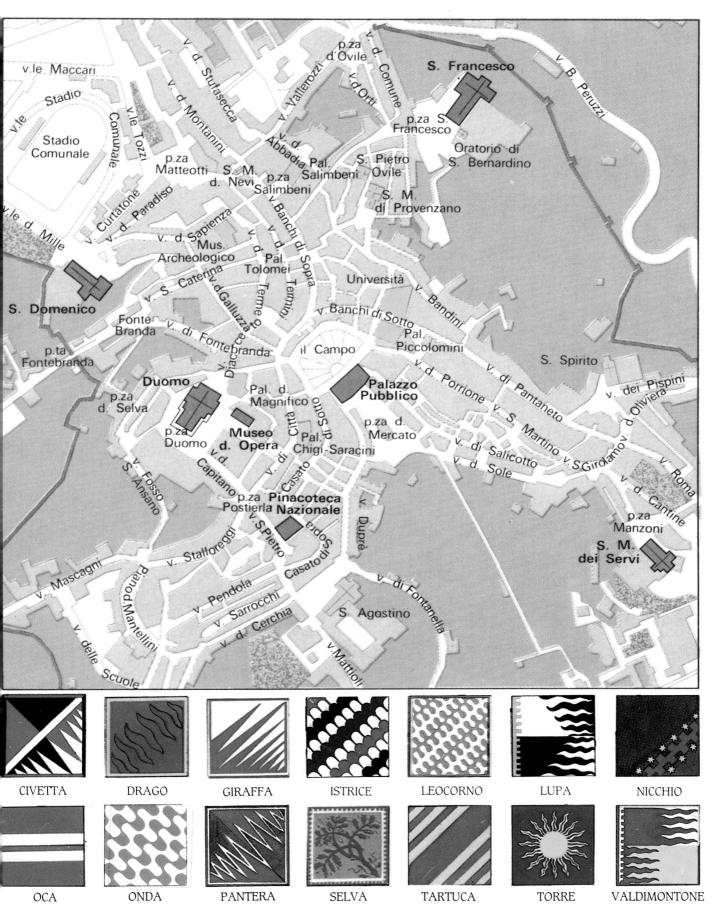

CIVETTA

DRAGO

GIRAFFA

ISTRICE

LEOCORNO

LUPA

NICCHIO

OCA

ONDA

PANTERA

SELVA

TARTUCA

TORRE

VALDIMONTONE

2nd ITINERARY: **Via di Città** of the Croce del Travaglio leads to **Piazza Postierla**. To the left, on Via San Pietro, is the **Pinacoteca Nazionale** and, to the right, the **Duomo** and the **Museo dell'Opera Metropolitana**.

1st ITINERARY

PIAZZA DEL CAMPO – Just «*Il Campo*» to the Sienese, the great fan-shaped square slopes down in the direction of Palazzo Pubblico. In the center of the brick paving is *Fonte Gaia,* adorned with sculpted reliefs by Jacopo della Quercia ranked among the masterpieces of 15th century art. (These, however, are copies; the originals are preserved inside Palazzo Pubblico.) Although the palaces and buildings bordering the square date from different periods (12th through 16th centuries), they nevertheless blend perfectly to form a harmonious whole. The most famous are *Palazzo Sansedoni* with its tower and three registers of Gothic three part windows, the *De Metz houses,* and *Palazzo d'Elci.*

PALAZZO PUBBLICO – Built, like Florence's Palazzo Vecchio, around the late 1200s, Palazzo Pubblico conveys an effect of major airiness for a variety of reasons: curvature of the facade, more color contrast, wide use of Gothic windows, and the vertical emphasis of the tower. The original architect is not known (Agostino di Giovanni or Agnolo di Ventura are two names advanced), although much of the design is actually due to later alterations and additions. The building is not only Siena's city hall but also a museum.

On the left side of the building is the *Torre del Mangia* designed by Lippo Memmi and built by Agostino di Giovanni around 1340. On top of the brick tower is a stone bell chamber where a certain Giovanni di Duccio nicknamed *Il Mangia* would sound the hours sometime in the 14th century. Il Mangia's job was later taken over by a mechanized figure (up to the 18th century), but the name stuck. Below the tower is the *Cappella di Piazza,* built between 1352 and 1376 in thanksgiving for deliverance from a plague epidemic. On the second floor is the entrance to the **Museo Civico.** In the museum lobby are remains of a fresco by Ambrogio Lorenzetti. On the right in the *Sala del Mappamondo* are two of Simone Martini's masterpieces: frescoes of the *Maestà* dated 1315 and *Guidoriccio da Fogliano* (depicted during the siege of Montemassi) dated 1328. Executed with a remarkable eye for pattern and line, they are among the outstanding example of the notably refined Sienese style of the 14th century. On the right is the *Sala della Pace* featuring a famous fresco cycle painted by Ambrogio Lorenzetti around 1340, with scenes showing *Good Government,* the *Effects of Good Government* and the *Effects of Bad Government.* The next room, *Sala dei Pilastri,* features works by Neroccio and followers of Duccio. Returning to the Sala del Mappamondo go left into the *Anticappella* and *Cappella,* adorned with paintings by Taddeo di Bartolo and Sodoma. From the Anticappella proceed to the *Sala dei Cardinali,* and then the *Sala del Concistoro* with a Rossellino portal (1448), frescoes, and 16th century tapestries. Cross the Sala dei Cardinali on your way to the *Sala di Balia,* adorned with 15th century frescoes. The following rooms feature collections of bronzes, ceramics, and coins. Upstairs in the *Loggia* are the original Jacopo della Quercia reliefs from the *Fonte Gaia* (dated c. 1415).

SAN DOMENICO – This impressive brick church in the Gothic style was built between the 13th and 15th centuries, whereas its belltower dates from 1340. The aisleless interior is divided by chapels. On the right side just beyond the entrance is the *Cappella delle Volte* with a late 14th century fresco of *St. Catherine of Siena* (believed to be a portrait) by Andrea Vanni. *Scenes from St. Catherine's life* were frescoed by Sodoma in 1526 in the *Cappella di Santa Caterina.* At the end of the right side is an *Adoration of the Shepherds* by Francesco di Giorgio. On the main altar is a ciborium with two *angels* carved by Benedetto da Maiano in 1475. On the left side are frescoes by Matteo di Giovanni and, on the fourth altar, a painting by Pietro Lorenzetti depicting the *Virgin with St. George and a knight.*

SAN FRANCESCO – A Baroque building with a modern facade, San Francesco was originally a medieval building (1326-1475). The aisleless interior has striped marble walls. Among the highlights are two

Aerial view of the town; below: the Cappella di Piazza (Chapel of the Square), at the foot of the Mangia Tower, that was built to fulfill a vow made during a plague epidemic.

The Palazzo Pubblico, with the tall Mangia Tower; below: two views of the new Fonte Gaia.

PALAZZO PUBBLICO - The Chapel inside the palace, attributed to Domenico di Niccolò; below: Guidoriccio da Fogliano at the siege of Montemassi, attributed to Simone Martini.

MUSEUM OF THE CATHEDRAL - Madonna and Child enthroned with angels and saints, Duccio di Buoninsegna's famous masterpiece; below: the exterior and interior of the Basilica of San Domenico.

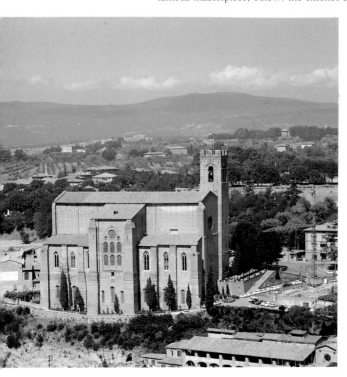 

paintings by Ambrogio Lorenzetti (*St. Louis Anjou and Boniface VIII* and the *Martyrdom of Franciscan Monks in Ceuta*) in the third lefthand transept and a *Crucifixion* by Pietro Lorenzetti in the first chapel on the right.

PALAZZO PICCOLOMINI – One of the most elegant examples of Renaissance civic architecture extant, the palace was begun under the supervision of Pietro Paolo del Porrina in 1469. The original design is traditionally ascribed to Bernardo Rossellino.

The building is now the state archives. Many of the documents (decrees, papal bulls, autographs, and illuminated manuscripts) are of historical interest. Especially noteworthy are the so-called *Tavolette di Biccherna*, wooden covers for the Sienese state's official ledgers, adorned with paintings of various subjects (13th-17th centuries).

SANTA MARIA DEI SERVI – Built in the 13th century, the church was considerably restored in the 15th and 16th centuries, especially in the nave area which is a fine example of Renaissance architecture. The most noteworthy of the paintings on display are a Byzantine style *Virgin and Child* by Coppo di Marcovaldo dated 1261 (second righthand altar), a fresco of the *Slaughter of the Innocents* by Pietro Lorenzetti, and the *Madonna del Popolo Altarpiece* by Lippo Memmi (both in the second righthand chapel of the choir). There are also frescoes by Lorenzetti (*Banquet of Herod* and *St. John the Evangelist*) in the second lefthand chapel of the choir. In the end chapel of the left transept is Giovanni di Paolo's *Madonna del Manto* dated 1436.

2nd ITINERARY

VIA DI CITTÀ – The slightly sloping street is flanked by superb palaces. Along the first stretch is the *Loggia della Mercanzia*, a 15th century building with strong Gothic overtones, designed by Sano di Matteo and Pietro del Minella. The statues in the niches represent *saints*. Proceeding, you pass *Palazzo Chigi-Saracini*, a 13th century building at no. 89, now the *Accademia Musicale Chigiana*, *Palazzo Piccolomini delle Papesse*, designed by Rossellino around 1465 at no. 126, and a Gothic palace, *Palazzo Marsili*, dated 1458, at no. 132 (among others).

PINACOTECA NAZIONALE – The museum building (*Palazzo Buonsignori*) is an elegant Gothic-style 15th century brick palace. The collection, focusing mainly on Sienese art between the 12th and 17th centuries, was begun in the late 1700s by an abbot, Giuseppe Ciaccheri.

Only the highlights will be mentioned. Room I (third floor) features 12th century Sienese works, e.g., *Transfiguration* and *scenes from the life of Christ* by Guido da Siena and an altarpiece depicting the *Savior* and other *New Testament scenes* dated 1215. Room II: *St. John the Baptist and scenes from his life*, late 13th century Sienese school, *St. Peter enthroned* attributed to Guido da Siena. Rooms III and IV: *Virgin and Child, St. Augustine and other saints*, and the delightful *Madonna dei Francescani*, three masterpieces by Duccio da Buoninsegna. Room VI: a celebrated *Virgin and Child* by Simone Martini. Room VII: a sampling of works by Ambrogio Lorenzetti, e.g., *Annunciation* (1344), the *Virgin and Child with saints, angels, and church fathers*, plus two panel paintings, one of a *castle by a lake* and the other of a *city near the seashore*, the earliest known Italian landscapes. In addition, there is an altarpiece by Pietro Lorenzetti depicting the *Virgin and Child with St. Nicholas and the Prophet Elijah* and *scenes of life in a Carmelite monastery* on the predella (1329). Room IX: paintings by Domenico di Bartolo and Michelino da Besozzo. Room XIII: *St. Anthony Abbot being beaten by devils* and *Last Supper* by Sassetta. Room XIV: *Virgin and Child with saints* by Neroccio and *Annunciation* by Francesco di Giorgio. Room XVIII: works by Sano di Pietro.

CATHEDRAL – The Duomo rose in the mid-1100s on the site of a preexisting 9th-10th century church. In Roman times, a temple dedicated to Minerva stood on this same hillside. In 1339, when the project (a concerted effort of the finest 13th and 14th century

The exterior of the noble Piccolomini Palace, at present headquarters of the State Archives; below: the Chigi Saracini Palace in Via di Città.

The National Picture Gallery (Pinacoteca Nazionale),
in Via San Pietro.

NATIONAL PICTURE GALLERY - Madonna of Humility, by Domenico di
Bartolo;below: detail from a Last Judgement, by Giovanni di Paolo;
left: detail of a Madonna and Child, by Neroccio di Bartolommeo.

architects) was nearing completion, it was decided to enlarge the original plan: the existing building would be just the transept of a «*Duomo Nuovo*» (new cathedral). Plague and economic political setbacks caused the gigantic project to be abandoned (and ensuing return to the original plans). Works was finished in the late 1300s.

The lower section of the facade with three Romanesque-Gothic *portals* is by Giovanni Pisano (1284-1296), (except for the relief of the central portal architrave which are by Tino di Camaino). The upper section, a 14th century work, was inspired by the Duomo of Orvieto; the cusp mosaics, on the other hand, are 19th century works. The interior is quite impressive: striped marble pillars set off the nave from the single aisles and the floor is alive with stupendous mosaics of *biblical scenes* executed in the 14th through 16th centuries by prominent Sienese artists. The church is a treasure-house of art masterpieces. Starting from the rightand transept: *Cappella Chigi* built by Bernini for Pope Alexander VII. On the main altar, designed by Peruzzi, is a ciborium by Vecchietta, while two of the flanking statues are by Francesco di Giorgio. A circular *stained glass window* designed by Duccio in 1288 illuminates the apse. At the left transept crossing is one of the masterpieces of Italian Gothic sculpture, the *pulpit* carved by Nicola Pisano (with the help of his son Giovanni and Arnolfo di Cambio) in 1268. In the nearby *Cappella di Sant'Ansano* is the *tomb of Cardinal Petroni* which Tino di Camaino carved in 1318. At the end of the transept, on the lefthand side, is the *Cappella di San Giovanni Battista*, a Renaissance design by Giovanni di Stefano (1482), which contains several notable works including Pinturicchio's *portrait of Alberto Aringhieri*, his *Birth of St. John the Baptist*, and a bronze *statue of St. John* sculpted by Donatello in 1487. From the left aisle enter the **Libreria Piccolomini**, built between the late 15th-early 16th centuries as the personal library of the Piccolomini pope, Pius II, with Pinturicchio frescoes, illuminated manuscripts, and the celebrated *Three Graces*, a Roman copy of a Greek original. In the nave is the *Piccolomini Altar* by Andrea Bregno (with some impressive figures, youthful works by Michelangelo, in the niches). On the right side of the Duomo you can see the remains of the unfinished *Duomo Nuovo*. Then walk down to the 14th century **Baptistry** which has a superb *baptismal font* by Jacopo della Quercia (1417), as well as sculptures by Donatello, Ghiberti, and others. Opposite is a Renaissance palace, *Palazzo del Magnifico*, built in 1508 for Pandolfo Petrucci called the "Magnificent".

MUSEO DELL'OPERA METROPOLITANA – Founded in 1870, the collection features works originally part of the Cathedral or Baptistry decoration.

Among the works in the ground floor *Salone* are ten *statues* by Giovanni Pisano (once part of the Duomo's facade), as well as a relief of the *Virgin and Child with St. Jerome and Cardinal Casini*, one of Jacopo della Quercia's finest sculptures. Duccio's *Maestà*, painted in 1311 for the main altar of the church, is displayed in a special room on the second floor. One of the great paintings of Western art, it is a complex work consisting of a great *Virgin Enthroned* panel (originally the front) plus 26 smaller panels (originally the back) depicting *scenes of the Passion*. In addition, the Maestà Room contains another *Virgin* by Duccio and the *Birth of the Virgin*, one of Pietro Lorenzetti's finest works (1342). Between the second and third floors is the *Sala del Tesoro* with an extensive collection of reliquaries, wood sculpture, and other fine crafted objects. On the third floor are Sienese school paintings after Duccio with works by Ambrogio Lorenzetti, Sodoma, Beccafumi, and Simone Martini who painted the striking *scenes from the life of Beato Agostino Novello* around 1330.

The wide nave of the Cathedral; below: the main altar.

Overall view of the Cathedral; below: a detail of the Choir-stalls; the Piccolomini Library, with the Pinturicchio frescoes.

THE ENVIRONS OF SIENA

1. Torri, San Galgano — 2. Monteriggioni — 3. L'Osservanza.

1. TORRI, SAN GALGANO

Leaving Siena, one proceeds in a south-westerly direction (through the Fontebranda gate) along state-road 73 towards Grosseto. At Malignano, a road off right leads to **Sovicille**, a Medieval castle, that, together with other manor-houses, monasteries and fortified farm-houses loosely linked to each other is situated on the Sienese **Montagnola**, a wooded, hilly, particularly picturesque area. Continuing along the state road, if one takes a road off left near Rosia, one reaches Torri.

TORRI – A fine avenue lined with cypresses leads up to this medieval hamlet, nestling against a Vallombrosan abbey, founded around the second half of the 13th century.

See the church of the Blessed Trinity (**Santissima Trinità**), that is flanked by a square cloister surrounded by three superimposed orders of loggias: the bottom order is in black and white marble with columns of differing shapes surmounted by beautifully carved capitals, the second has octagonal brick columns and the third has wooden columns.

Leaving the lush landscape of the Montagnola, the state road winds through the first foothills of the Colline Metallifere (Metalliferous Hills), while the landscape becomes wilder and more barren, as the Sienese countryside merges into the Maremma. At the Madonnino, the road forks and taking the right fork in the direction of Massa Marittima, one shortly finds a turning on the left leading towards San Galgano.

SAN GALGANO – Impressive ruins of one of the most noteworthy examples in Italy of Gothic-Cistercian architecture (together with the two other abbeys of Fossanova and Casamari in Latium).

The church dates back to the 13th century and belonged to an imposing abbey founded at the end of the 12th century by the Cistercian monks of Casamari (the Cistercian order was founded in Citeaux, in France), who based the design of the Abbey church on their Mother church of Citeaux, contributing in a vital manner towards the expansion of the Gothic style in Tuscany. The reason this site was chosen, was Galgano Guidotti, a 12th century nobleman of Chiusdino, who spent the latter part of his life as a hermit on Mount Siepi, the hill behind the abbey, choosing to be robed in a Cistercian habit on his death-bed. After centuries, during which it wielded great influence and power, becoming the most puissant abbey of the region, its fortunes started to wane, in the 15th century, and decline set in, in increasing measure, over the following centuries, until the final blow was dealt when religious institutions were suppressed and the monastery became a farm (1816). Damage was already visible in the 16th century, when vain attempts were made to repair them; in the 18th century the bell tower collapsed, followed by the roof of the abbey. The ground plan is a Latin cross with a nave separated from the side-aisles by robust cruciform pillars, with great ogival and mullioned windows along the massive flanks of the aisles (only one of the windows still has the column dividing it) the transept is tripartite too; the typically Cistercian rectangular apse is pierced by two lines of superimposed ogival windows and two round openings. Today, the beauty of the sky, the balanced harmony of the airy structure, the grassy floor, the happy blend of outdoor and inner beauty evoke a kind of Pan-like emotion, endowing the ruins with the sacred atmosphere normally associated with temples dedicated to Olympic deities. To the right of the church are the monastic buildings, where part of the cloisters are still standing, as well as the Chapter Hall — a vast chamber divided into two cross-vaulted naves, which has managed to preserve its original appearance. In 1967, the monastery was granted to a community of Mount Olive Benedictine nuns. Another architectural gem of the complex is the magnificent circular Romanesque *oratory* (an unusual shape in the Sienese architectural context), which stands atop nearby Monte Siepi. The church was finished in 1185, the year in which St. Gawain (Galgano) was canonised, just a few years after his death (1181); it was built above the place in which the saint used to pray, kneeling before his sword, that he had stuck into a rock, so that its hilt formed a cross (the rock is the original,

Torri - Above and below: two views of the typically Medieval burg.

San Galgano - The Romanesque Oratory.

San Galgano - The splendid interior of the Abbey church; below: a side-aisle and the exterior.

legendary one, whereas the sword is fairly recent). The austere interior, of great beauty, opens onto a little chapel added in the 14th century, decorated with frescoes by Ambrogio Lorenzetti.

2. MONTERIGGIONI

Monteriggioni suddenly appears to ones left, at the top of a hill, when one is driving northwards along the Florence superstrada from Siena.

MONTERIGGIONI – A typical medieval burg, completely surrounded by its turreted walls, built in the 13th century, enjoying a highly visible position atop its strategically placed hill.

The walls, with their fourteen square turrets, were mentioned by Dante in his *Inferno*. The Sienese constructed the town, at the beginning of the 14th century, as a garrison to protect the approaches to Siena during the period in which the Florentines were waging war against them. As one might expect, the atmosphere within the walls is of perfect Medieval stillness; the parish church of **Santa Maria**, a Romanesque Gothic structure, abuts on the main street that divides the town in half, lengthwise, connecting the two gates, one of which is on the Florence side, the other opening being cut into the lower part of one of the towers, on the Siena side.

About three kms. from Monteriggioni, is the burg of **Abbadia Isola**, a hamlet that grew up around the Cistercian abbey of San Salvatore (11th century). The place was named Isola (island), because it used to be surrounded by marshy land. The remains of the monastery are situated around a courtyard, together with the abbey church – a Lombard type structure built between the 11th and 13th centuries. The tripartite interior is set-off by three apses and contains a remarkable fresco depicting a *Madonna and Child enthroned*, by a follower of Duccio di Buoninsegna.

3. THE OSSERVANZA

Leaving Siena via the Ovile gate, one proceeds northwards along Via Simone Martini, then one follows the arrows until one gets to the Osservanza.

THE MONASTERY OF THE OSSERVANZA – A great Renaissance complex situated on the hill of the Capriola, commanding a magnificent view over Siena, founded, to start with, in the 13th century. St. Bernardino lived there.

In the second half of the 15th century, the construction of the monastery – attributed to Francesco di Giorgio Martini, one of the most distinguished architects in Renaissance Siena, as well as to one of his best assistants, Giacomo Cozzarelli – lasted until about 1490. The same two architects, somewhat later (1495-97), designed the sacristy and the crypt of the church, which the Lord of Siena, Pandolfo Petrucci, the promoter of further additions (such as the guest-house and the infirmary, etc.) desired as his family sepulchre, causing the monastery to achieve its moment of greatest splendour at the beginning of the 16th century. The church, that has been restored after the dreadful damage dealt to it during World War II, is completely made of brick. The aisleless interior with its eight side-chapels, dome and transept, contains remarkable works of art, such as a 15th century *reliquary* of St. Bernardino (third chapel on the right), a triptych depicting a *Madonna and Child with Saints*, by the so-called Master of the Osservanza (15th century) in the 4th chapel on the right, two glazed terracottas by Andrea della Robbia showing the *Archangel Gabriel* and the *Virgin Annunciate* (end of 15th century) beneath the triumphal arch of the nave and by the same artist, a great panel in glazed terracotta depicting the *Coronation of the Virgin* (second chapel on the left); the terracotta and stucco medallions on the ceiling vault are by Andrea della Robbia and Giacomo Cozzarelli, who also shaped the fine *Deposition* in the sacristy. The **museum** next door, named after **Aurelio Castelli**, is also worth a visit and contains a collection of various works of art, originally in the church.

Monteriggioni - The parish church of Santa Maria.

The church and monastery of the Osservanza.
Sienese landscape.

Monteriggioni - View of the 14th century walls surrounding the Medieval burg. Below: the characteristic Sienese «Crete».

THE PROVINCE OF SIENA

The Castle of Brolio.

1. The Sienese Chianti — 2. Colle Val D'Elsa, San Gimignano — 3. The "Crete", Montalcino and the Amiata — 4. San Quirico d'Orcia, Pienza, Montepulciano, Chiusi.

1. The Sienese Chianti

The itinerary traverses the southern part of the Chianti district (see also Itinerary 5 in the Province of Florence). The feature the whole of this area has in common, is no precise geographical boundary provided by the geological conformation of the area, but the extraordinary quality of the wine produced on its slopes. The areas of Radda, Gaiole and Castellina (the "historical" core of the wine producing territory, already famous in the Middle Ages), followed by the neighbouring territories bordered by San Casciano, San Gimignano, Montepulciano, Montalcino and beyond, formed a consortium in 1924, adopting the ancient badge of a Chianti league as their crest: the black rooster. Three years later, the name of Chianti was granted to vine-growers outside the "black rooster" area, and the consortium of the "Putto" (babe or cherub) was founded (Pisan, Arretine, Florentine hills, Montalbano and Rufina). In southern Chianti, too, farms and country market towns stud the landscape together with a considerable number of castles: vivid reminders of the land's feudal past.

Leaving Siena via the Ovile gate, one proceeds in a north-easterly direction along twisty road Nr. 408, in the direction of Montevarchi. At the crossroads with road Nr. 484, one turns right along the latter and one comes to Brolio.

CASTLE OF BROLIO – Situated on a hilltop, at the end of a cypress-lined avenue, it is one of the most lovely manor-houses in Tuscany.

It already existed in the 9th century (Brolio is a name of Longobard origin and means "orchard") and has belonged to the Ricasoli family since the middle of the 12th century. For centuries the castle witnessed, and at times was a victim of, the innumerable wars between Florence and Siena. In the 19th century the castle was heavily restored by order of Bettino Ricasoli, the "iron Baron", the dictator of Tuscany — after the fall of the Hapsburg-Lorraine family — who was Cavour's successor as head of the government of the Kingdom of Italy; he was also an esteemed agronomist and contributed in a vital fashion towards the establishment of the wine-producing rules at the basis of the production of true Chianti wine. In the castle, one can visit the 14th century **Chapel of San Jacopo** (St. James), containing a polyptych by Ugolino di Nerio, and, in the crypt, the Ricasoli family sepulchre; the keep with the sentry's walk; the sumptuous lordly apartments and, naturally, the cellars.

The Castle of Meleto.
The Castle of Barbischio.

Returning to state road Nr. 408, one proceeds along it until one encounters the **Castle of Meleto**, which was built around the year 1000, which was involved in innumerable war-like adventures, like Brolio; it belonged to the Firidolfi and Ricasoli families and witnessed the passage of Charles V's Imperial army, on its way to conquer Siena in 1536. It experienced a felicitous moment in the 18th century, when the halls were frescoed and a charming private theatre was built inside the castle, still in excellent condition. The castle estate is a major producer of "Black Rooster" Chianti. Just a little further on, one comes to **Gaiole**, an ancient market town that grew up in the vicinity of the estate of one Gaio (whence the name). From Gaiole one can visit two fine castles: **Vertine** and **Barbischio**.

One proceeds up to the fork, the left branch of which leads to Badia a Coltibuono.

BADIA A COLTIBUONO – The church and a few picturesque chambers belonging to the once powerful, ancient abbey survive as part of a farm.

Founded in the 8th century, it was completely rebuilt by the Benedictine Vallombrosan monks in the 12th century and again in the 15th-16th centuries, when a number of halls, such as the refectory, the library and the dormitory corridor were frescoed. The fine Romanesque church has an octagonal dome and a massive 13th century belltower.

Returning to the fork where one meets state road Nr. 408, one turns right onto road Nr. 429 to get to **Radda**. Only a few sections of the ancient fortified burg's

Three views of the magnificent vineyards in the Sienese countryside, where one produces the famous Black Rooster Chianti appreciated all over the world for its unmistakable quality.

walls are still standing. Once domain of the Counts Guidi, and the Florentine garrison defended strenuously by Francesco Ferrucci, it contains the well-preserved 15th century **Praetorian Palace**, decorated with the badges of the podestà who resided within its walls. Opposite the palace, a flight of steps leads up to the church of **San Niccolò**, with its elegant, frescoed Gothic façade. To name but a few of the castles in the environs of Radda, let one not omit **Monterinaldi**, that dates as far back as the times of the Etruscans, **Volpaia** and **Albola**. The road continues through enchanting countryside until one reaches Castellina.

CASTELLINA IN CHIANTI
– An important agricultural centre and holiday resort, it is situated at the top of a hill, commanding excellent views down the valleys of the Pesa, Arbia and Elsa rivers.

One of the earliest events to have affected this town of Etruscan origins, was the raid of Gaulish invaders that destroyed it. The town was fortified by the Counts Guidi and belonged later on to the Lords of Trebbio and later still to Florence. As headquarters of the League of the Chianti, it was once more destroyed, at the end of the 14th century, by the Sienese. In the course of the following century, it was rebuilt, enlarged and fortified by Florence, only to be once more razed to the ground, this time by the Aragonese, allied to Siena (1478). The buildings of greatest interest include: the massive, battlemented Fortress (**Rocca**), now housing the Municipal Offices and a small **Etruscan Museum**; the curious **Via delle Volte**, a fortified gangway lit by narrow, slit-like embrasures that offer magnificent glimpses of the surrounding country-side; the **parish church** with a fresco by Lorenzo di Bicci.

2. COLLE VAL D'ELSA, SAN GIMIGNANO

From Siena, one takes the Florence superstrada leaving it via the exit marked Colle Val d'Elsa.

COLLE VAL D'ELSA
– A town of considerable historical, artistic and industrial interest, situated on the left bank of the Elsa, divided into two parts: Colle Basso or the Piano, in the valley, where all the factories and modern housing developments are; and Colle Alto, at the top of the hill, with its typically Medieval structure.

It was a Free Commune in the 12th century, and a bone of contention for both Sienese and Florentines. In 1333 Colle surrendered to Florence. During the 9th century it had already become an industrial centre: the first activities to prosper in Colle were the paper-mills, thanks to the energy supplied by the waters of the Elsa. The same waters, by means of a complex system of canals, were also instrumental in the development of another industrial alternative that flourished in the town: crystal grinding. (Colle is still nicknamed the "Bohemia of Italy"). In the 15th century it started developing its printing establishments. The centre of Colle Basso is the square named after the most famous son of the town: Arnolfo di Cambio, the famous sculptor and architect. On the banks of the Elsa, one comes across the **Badia di Spugna**, now a farm, where one can however still glimpse a few traces of the first and most important church in Colle. Also on the plain (Piano), one can see the 13th century church of **Sant'Agostino**. A tree-lined avenue mounts up to Colle Alto. The nucleus of the high town is surrounded by walls that protect its numerous lovely buildings, such as the 16th century **Palazzo Campana**, designed by Giuliano di Baccio d'Agnolo (1539). Through a wide arch on one side of Palazzo Campana, one enters the **Castle**, which used to be the ancient fortified burg of Piticciano, later incorporated by the township of Colle; picturesque Via del Castello, lined with tower-mansions and other Medieval buildings, leads into the Cathedral square, where one finds the 14th century **Praetorian Palace**, which has become the headquarters of an **Antiquarium**, containing a rich collection of Etruscan and Roman finds from all over the Val d'Elsa. The early 17th century **Cathedral** contains a *Nativity*, by Rutilio Manetti, an elegant *bronze lectern* by Tacca in the Chapel of the Chiodo (Nail), a bronze *Crucifix*, attributed to Giambologna, upon the main altar, a *Communion of St. Mary of Egypt*, by Pollaiolo and a 15th century *pulpit*, by Benedetto da Maiano. Proceeding along Via del Castello, one encounters the **Civic Museum**, the Medieval **Theatre of the Varii**, and the **tower mansion of Arnolfo di Cambio** (early 13th century). See also a curiously picturesque Medieval tunnel-alley, called the **Via delle Volte**, that burrows its way under the town for about 100 ms.

From Colle Val d'Elsa, state road Nr. 68 towards Volterra leads one into **Castel San Gimignano**, a medieval fortified burg, then one bears right towards San

Badia a Coltibuono.

Radda - The Praetorian Palace, below: the church of San Niccolò.

Colle Val d'Elsa - The centre of Colle Basso. Below, left: **Castellina** - The Fort.

Colle Val d'Elsa - View; below: the 13th century walls.

Gimignano, choosing the fine road that cuts through **San Donato**, with its Romanesque parish church.

SAN GIMIGNANO

SAN GIMIGNANO – One of the most unique Tuscan towns, thanks to its severely Medieval aspect (bristling with tall towers and protected by its perfectly intact fortifications). Most prosperous during the 12th and 13th centuries, when it enjoyed the status of Free Commune (frequently at war with Volterra and devoured by internecine strife), it finally surrendered to Florence in 1354.

The most typical product of its carefully tended slopes is an excellent white wine, known as *Vernaccia*, one of the best in Tuscany. From spacious Piazza Martiri di Monte Maggio, one enters the walled town via *Porta San Giovanni*, the gate cut into the 13th century walls, and climbs up Via San Giovanni, flanked by ancient mansions, towards the centre of the town. Passing beneath the Arco dei Becci, one emerges into the wide, triangular **Piazza della Cisterna**, that derives its name from the *cisterna* (well - 13th/14th cent.) in the middle of the square, which is surrounded by ancient buildings, such as *Palazzo Tortoli* and the two *Ardinghelli towers*. Continuing onwards, one comes to the **Cathedral square**: the **Palazzo del Podestà** (13th/14th cent.) is to ones right, with its loggia and a high tower, called the *Rognosa*, the latter flanked by the 13th century *Chigi Tower*; opposite, one espies the two *Salvucci towers*; to the left, at the top of a high flight of steps, is the **Collegiata** (Cathedral), a Romanesque building, restructured in the 15th century by Giuliano da Maiano. The interior, with a nave flanked by two side-aisles, contains a rich selection of works of art: the inner façade and the first part of the upper nave walls are decorated with frescoes depicting the *Last Judgement*: the *Paradise* and *Hell* scenes are by Taddeo di Bartolo (1393), beneath the Judgement scenes, is the *Martyrdom of St. Sebastian*, by Benozzo Gozzoli; the walls of the left aisle are frescoed with scenes from the *Old Testament* by Bartolo di Fredi c. 1367), whereas the walls of the right aisle are decorated with frescoed scenes from the *New Testament* (by Barna da Siena, c. 1350); at the end of the right aisle one finds the splendid **Chapel of St. Fina**, a masterpiece by Benedetto and Giuliano da Maiano (1468) frescoed with *Episodes from the Life of the Saint*, by Ghirlandaio; the *Annunciation* frescoed on the end wall of the outside loggia, to the left of the Cathedral, is also attributed to the Circle of Ghirlandaio. On the southern side of the Cathedral square is the **Palazzo del Popolo** (People's Palace - end of the 13th century), where one can admire the **Civic Museums** (Maestà, by Lippo Memmi) and the Picture Gallery (**Pinacoteca**), which one reaches by climbing up to the upper floors via the charming little inner courtyard; the Picture Gallery contains interesting works by Florentine and Sienese masters: a *Crucifix*, by Coppo di Marcovaldo, two tondi, by Filippino Lippi, paintings by Benozzo Gozzoli, Bartolo di Fredi and Mainardi. From the square, one continues down the picturesque Via San Matteo (the *Pesciolini tower-mansion* - end of the 13th century), until one reaches a great Romanesque-Gothic church of the end of the 13th century: **Sant'Agostino**, which contains an *altar* by Benedetto da Maiano and exceptional frescoes by Benozzo Gozzoli (in the apse), depicting episodes from the *Life of St. Augustine*. The **Rocca** (Fortress - 14th century) commands the superb view at the top of the town.

3. THE "CRETE", MONTALCINO AND THE AMIATA

Leaving Siena via the Pispini gate, one proceeds in a south-easterly direction, for a brief stretch along state road 326 in the direction of Sinalunga, then one bears right, along state road 438 towards **Asciano** which one gets to, after a few kilometers of the evocative landscape of the "crete", which are fissured ruts and irregularities caused by the erosion of the limestone terrain, characterised by an almost total absence of trees; on the horizon, towards the south, one catches occasional glimpses of the conical shape of Mount Amiata. Just before one reaches Asciano, where one can visit an interesting **Etruscan Museum**, a Museum of Religious Art (**Museo di Arte Sacra**) and a Romanesque church called the **Collegiata**, a road off right leads back to the Via Cassia, passing through Monte Oliveto.

MONTE OLIVETO – The red brick used for the construction of this famous abbey draws the eye amidst the bare, clay-coloured hills of the "Crete". Of great artistic interest, the monastery, that was absorbed into the Benedictine Order, was founded in 1313 by a Sienese, Bernardo Tolomei and continued to expand until the 18th century.

San Gimignano - Via San Giovanni; below: the Podestà's Palace seen from above.

San Gimignano - Overall view with the characteristic towers.

CHAPEL OF SANTA FINA (in the Cathedral) - Above and below: two episodes from the Life of Saint Fina, by Domenico del Ghirlandaio.

San Gimignano - The Collegiata Cathedral; below: the interior.

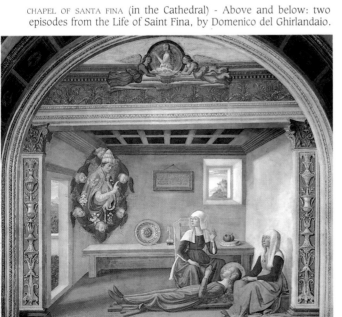

San Gimignano - The courtyard of the Palace of the Commune; CIVIC MUSEUM - Saint Gimignano blessing the town on his lap, detail from a panel of the altar-piece by Taddeo di Bartolo.

CIVIC MUSEUM - One of the rooms; left: Virgin in Glory with Saints, by Pinturicchio; below: fresco attributed to Memmo di Filippuccio.

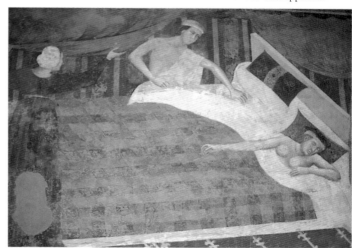

San Gimignano - Piazza della Cisterna; below: the Fort, seen from the tower of the Palace of the Commune.

One enters the complex via the great tower gate belonging to a kind of 14th-15th century guard-house, continuing down a cypress-lined avenue to the church, that was constructed towards the beginning of the 15th century and underwent restructuring in the 18th, so that only the portal and the belltower remain of the original structure. The most fascinating part of the monastic complex is the great cloister, with its magnificent cycle of frescoes depicting *Episodes from the Life of St. Benedict* (late 15th, early 16th cents.), by Luca Signorelli and Sodoma, representing one of the most splendid instances of Renaissance art in Italy. From the great cloister, one walks through an archway [beneath which one can admire two more frescoes by Sodoma, based on the Passion of Christ (fine *Christ at the Column*)] and enters a hallway, decorated with other frescoes by Sienese artists, leading into the pompous Baroque abbey-church which contains the marvellous carved and inlaid choir-stalls made at the beginning of the 16th century by Friar Giovanni da Verona. See also the middle cloister and the charming little cloister (mid- 15th cent.), the refectory and the fine 1518 library.

One makes ones way towards Buonconvento, on the Cassia (state road 2), then one continues southwards until Torrenieri, where one turns right, to get to Montalcino.

MONTALCINO

MONTALCINO – An agricultural centre situated at the top of a hill covered with olive groves and vineyards, overlooking the two valleys of the Ombrone and Asso rivers, renowned for its Brunello Moscadello wines, which is one of the most interesting places in the Sienese province.

In the middle of the town, with its typical late Medieval aspect, with visible traces of the Sienese domination, is the Piazza del Popolo, where one finds the **Communal Palace**, built between the 13th and 14th centuries together with its great adjoining Gothic 14th-15th century loggia. Not far off, is the church of **Sant'Egidio** (the interior of which was completely restructured in the 17th century), rebuilt by the Sienese in 1325 upon the foundations of a pre-esisting Romanesque building, of which traces are left in the new Gothic structure. The church of **Sant'Agostino** (14th century) is another Romanesque-Gothic church; the aisleless interior contains frescoes by Sienese 14th century masters. The **Diocesan Museum** and the **Civic Museum** are both extremely interesting, inasmuch as both contain admirable 14th and 15th century paintings of the Sienese School, as well as fine examples of the minor arts. The **Archaeological Museum**, arranged inside the old dispensary of the hospital of Santa Maria della Croce, contains important prehistoric and Etruscan objects from the surroundings. The five-sided Fortress (**Rocca** - 14th century) commands the top of the hill above the town; one can visit the interior and taste and buy the famous local wines (the celebrated *Brunello* is not to be missed) in the Wine Cellars (Enoteca) arranged on the ground-floor.

From Montalcino a road leads southwards to the Amiata, passing through **Sant'Antimo**. This solitary abbey, a few kilometres from Montalcino, is a Tuscan Romanesque architectural jewel. The ancient splendour of the Benedictine order (the abbey is supposed to have been founded in the 9th century at Charlemagne's command) is reflected in the magnificently powerful lines of the 12th century Romanesque-Cistercian abbey church, with its massive Lombard-type belltower; the plain façade boasts the fine sculpted Romanesque portal (the architrave bears the name of one of the architects: Azzone dei Porcari), whilst a smaller 11th century door can be admired on the left side of the church; the tripartite airy interior possesses fine columns and pillars with elaborate capitals, some of which are made of onyx; the semi-circular apse opens onto an ambulatory leading into radiating chapels (from the outside one can appreciate the purity of the structural lines); the fine mullioned openings of the matronei (women's galleries) run along the walls of the nave beneath the rafters of the beamed ceiling; underneath the church is a crypt that dates back, in all likelihood, to the 11th century. The **Amiata**, a solitary spent volcano, with its flanks covered by beech trees and chestnut woods stands between the valleys of the Orcia, Fiora and Paglia rivers. The landscape, with its lush vegetation and bubbling springs is an ideal spot for summer outings. In the area around **Abbadia San Salvatore**, there are numerous skiing establishments, much frequented during the winter.

4. SAN QUIRICO D'ORCIA, PIENZA, MONTEPULCIANO, CHIUSI

Leaving Siena, one proceeds southwards along the Via Cassia (state road Nr. 2) until San Quirico.

Asciano - The Collegiata of Sant'Agata.

Monteoliveto - The 16th century fish-pool, in the Monastic complex.

Montalcino - The towers of the Communal Palace and of the church of Sant'Agostino.

Monteoliveto - The entrance to the Abbey, with the enamelled terracotta relief, by the Della Robbia workshop, above the arch of the gateway; the apse of the church.

Montalcino - The 14th century Fort and view. Below: **Monte Amiata** - Two views.

SAN QUIRICO D'ORCIA – A prevalently agricultural town situated on the Via Cassia, in a position high-up above the Orcia and Asso valleys.

High Medieval documents refer to the place as San Quirico in Osenna, or Ausinna, Nosenna or Rosenna; in the 12th century, it was the seat of an Imperial Delegate (Vicar), thereafter, from the middle of the following century, it was ruled over by Siena, whose fortunes it shared, until it was incorporated into the Medici State in the 16th century. From an artistic point of view, it possesses a highly interesting historical nucleus, centred around the magnificent **Collegiata** (Cathedral, which was restored after the damage it sustained during the last conflict), a Romanesque edifice of the 12th/13th centuries, that was built above a pre-existing 8th century structure. The monumental portal on the plain façade is Romanesque, dated 1080, framed by an arched porch of extreme elegance, supported by double knotted columns held up by crouching lionesses (lovely relief above the architrave showing fighting dragons or monsters). The portal on the right flank, dated around the second half of the 13th century, has a remarkable, Lombard-looking structure, carved by a pupuil of Giovanni Pisano (see the caryatids supported by lions holding up the porch). The latest portal (the architrave is dated 1298) is the Gothic one that leads into the right arm of the transept. The aisleless interior contains a triptych by Sano di Pietro (*Madonna and Child enthroned with Saints*) and lovely choir-stalls by Antonio Barili. Just behind the Collegiata is **Palazzo Chigi**, an austere 17th century construction, designed by Carlo Fontana, which was much damaged during World War II. The fortifications of the town also surround a 16th century park, known as the **Orti Leonini**, founded around 1581 thanks to the wishes of Diomede Leoni (whence the name -- the definition Orti was used at the time to indicate important gardens, like the Orti Oricellari, in Florence or the Orti Farnesiani in Rome). The unusual aspect of this garden, was the fact that it was designed as a place in which the passing pilgrims and travellers could seek rest and peace, in other words as a public park, which it still is today, and not as a palace garden or private delight. It covers an irregular shaped area and is still, as it originally was, divided into two areas: the Italianate garden, with box-hedged beds arranged concentrically around the centrally placed statue of Cosimo III de' Medici and a "wild" "boschetto" of ilexes dividing the formal garden from a spacious field that surrounds the area on which the Medieval Keep (**Cassero**) used to stand, before it was destroyed during the last war.

Not far from San Quirico (proceed southwards, then take the turning leading off right from the Cassia) is the picturesque hot springs watering place of **Bagno Vignoni**, renowned since ancient times for the healing powers of its bicarbonate-sulphate-alcaline-terrous waters (52°C), of great benefit against rheumatic and arthritic afflictions (even Lorenzo the Magnificent came here, in 1490). The great swimming pool built around the hot springs in the centre of the main square of the town is the most picturesque and distinctive feature of the place: the walled pool, that one would expect to find surrounded by the fronds of a carefully arranged garden, here replaces the paving stones of what would elsewhere be the main square, reflecting the façades of the houses surrounding the steaming, misty vapours that cover the open-air hot-water-filled pool.

From San Quirico, one proceeds eastwards along state road Nr. 146, which winds through an extremely attractive landscape towards the Valdichiana, passing through some of the most beautiful Medieval towns in Tuscany.

PIENZA – Commanding a magnificent view from the ridge of a hill situated between the Orcia and Asso valleys, it is the physical embodiment of the "ideal city" described and debated over for years by the architects, and town-planners of the Renaissance.

Both Enea Silvio Piccolomini — who became a pope, assuming the name of Pius II (whence the name Pienza) and who decided to embellish his native town, known up to that moment as Corsignano — as well as Bernardo Rossellino — a genius of an architect, and pupil to Leon Battista Alberti, who was given the task, in 1459, of transforming the little village into a noble little town — deserve to share the merit of creating this jewel. Rossellino based his plans on Alberti's ideas and completely restructured the lay-out of the town, providing it with a totally new main square: the magnificent **Piazza Pio II**, surrounded by lovely architectural masterpieces: the **Communal Palace** (1463), opposite the Cathedral, is entirely built in travertine (except for the two-storeyed battlemented tower, in brick), with a loggia and twin-mullioned windows on the upper floor. Left of the Cathedral is the **Bishop's Palace**, estwhile Palazzo Borgia, as one can infer from the badge of the Borgia family on the corner of the building, which used to be a Gothic building, but was restored by Cardinal Rodrigo

Bagno Vignoni - The Baths.

San Quirico d'Orcia - The Orti Leonini.
Pienza - City Gate.

San Quirico d'Orcia - View.

The Sienese Countryside.
Pienza - View.

Borgia (later pope Alexander VI). The Cathedral was built between 1459 and 1462, upon designs by Rossellino; the fine Renaissance façade of travertine, that reminds one irresistibly of Alberti's lines, delights the eye with its three, harmonious arches, supported by columns, surmounted by a tympanum bearing the Piccolomini crest at its centre; there are two niches above the side doors, whereas a round opening surmounts the central doorway. The elegant interior is tripartite, the height of the nave being identical to that of the aisles, the ceiling is cross-vaulted and five chapels radiate off the apse, where one can admire Vecchietta's *Assumption*, the 1462 wooden choir-stalls and other works of considerable interest. The **Cathedral Museum**, next door, contains paintings, tapestries, miniatures and golden artifacts of the 14th-16th centuries. To the right of the Cathedral is **Palazzo Piccolomini**, a marvellous creation by Rossellino (who also designed the 1462 well to one side of the façade), constructed between 1459 and 1462. Based on Alberti's designs for the Rucellai palace in Florence, it is a compact building of smooth, rusticated blocks with two orders of twin-mullioned windows lighting its upper storeys; the inner courtyard is composedly harmonious with its portico running around the perfect square of the court; the courtyard leads out into the lovely garden terrace, overlooking the valley, through a doorway in the southern wall. From the garden, one can admire the superb loggias, on three superimposed levels disposed across the southern flank of the palace. One can visit the first floor chambers, where there is a collection of memorabilia and works of art of varied nature.

Pienza - The Cathedral; below: the Communal Palace.

MONTEPULCIANO

MONTEPULCIANO – The town is situated at the top of a hill commanding the Valdichiana and the Val d'Orcia. It is renowned for its excellent wines, chief among which one must mention the Vino Nobile. The rich fabric of the town is made even more fascinating by the intricate network of steep, narrow, twisting alleyways, flanked on either side by buildings of a prevalently Renaissance-like flavour.

An ancient Etruscan settlement (according to the legend, it was founded by Lars Porsenna himself), it was mentioned in a document dated 715, as Mons Politianus. In the 13th century, it was conquered by Siena, becoming a Florentine dominion towards the middle of the 14th century. Angelo Ambrogini, known as Poliziano (1454-1494), the elegant, cultured poet of the Medici court, was born here; so was Cardinal Roberto Bellarmino 1532-1621), the zealous supporter of the Counter-Reformation, who was instrumental in encouraging the development of Baroque art, after the splendid flowering of the 16th century, which, in Montepulciano, led to the construction of buildings by famous artists, such as Sangallo, Vignola and others. Along the main street, **Via Roma**, flanked by 16th century buildings, we find **Palazzo Avignonesi**, a late-Renaissance building, attributed to Vignola, possessing two superimposed orders of elegant windows. Further on, one comes to the 15th century church of **Sant'Agostino**, by Michelozzo (who also made the fine terracotta relief above the portal) in which the Gothic influence is still apparent; the aisleless interior, restructured in the 18th century, contains a *San Bernardino da Siena*, by Giovanni di Paolo (15th century). Via Roma continues, under another name (Via Cavour) leading to **Palazzo Cervini**, dressed with rusticated stone blocks and designed by Antonio da Sangallo the Elder. In Via Garibaldi, one finds the **House of Poliziano** of the 14th-15th century, that has been restructured a number of times. The centre of the town in **Piazza Grande**, at the top of the hill, surrounded by fine buildings such as: the **Communal Palace** (14th-15th centuries) with a façade attributed to Michelozzo and a handsome inner courtyard (14th century); austere **Palazzo Contucci**, by Antonio da Sangallo the Elder; **Palazzo Tarugi**, attributed with some uncertainty either to Vignola or Antonio da Sangallo the Elder, with a double loggia, on the ground floor and on the upper storey; the **Cathedral**, a late-Renaissance work by Scalza (late 16th century) which contains sculptures by Michelozzo, which are the dismembered parts of a sepulchre that was dismantled in the 17th century, lost and finally rediscovered in the 19th century, together with a fine triptych depicting the *Assumption* (1401), by Taddeo di Bartolo. Not far off, we find **Civic Museum**, (works of the Florentine and Sienese Schools of the 13th-18th centuries). Just outside the town, one finds the church of **San Biagio** (St. Blaise), a masterpiece by Antonio da Sangallo the Elder (1518-1545) and a luminous example of Tuscan Renaissance architecture. The nearby **Canonica** (Rectory) (1595), designed by Sangallo is an extraordinarily harmonious construction, enhanced and given added airy elegance by its double loggia.

The road approaches the initial reaches of the Valdichiana, curving slightly to touch **Chianciano Terme**, after which one reaches Chiusi.

Chianciano Terme - View.

Pienza - Palazzo Piccolomini.

Montepulciano - The church of San Biagio, a masterpiece by Antonio da Sangallo, the Elder; below: the Communal Palace, with its façade attributed to Michelozzo.

Montepulciano - Palazzo Tarugi.
Chianciano Terme - Piazza Italia.

155

CHIUSI – An enormously ancient Etruscan settlement, perched above a tufaceous hill. Between the 7th and 5th centuries B.C., it enjoyed a period of great splendour, when its power constituted a threat for the nascent state of Rome and its Lucumon (king), Lars Porsenna, nearly defeated the Roman king, Tarquin the Pround.

There are a number of fine Etruscan tombs all over the area around the town, as well as a curious system of tunnels that runs beneath the streets of the whole town (some of them are still being used as cellars by the inhabitants of the houses above them). The street plan of Chiusi, on the other hand reflects the lines of a Roman military camp. One should, in effect, remember that Rome occupied Chiusi at the beginning of the 3rd century B.C.. During the Middle Ages, the town was ravaged by malaria, later still it was taken-over by Florence. The **Cathedral**, which dates back to the 6th century, was much restructured during the last century. In the interior, the columns that separate the nave from the side-aisles are all that is left of the Roman buildings once in Chiusi; underneath the bell tower there is a large chamber-probably of Roman construction (in all likelihood a cistern). Next to the Cathedral is the **National Etruscan Museum**. The material it contains mostly comes from sites around Chiusi; sculptures, bucchero vases, cinerary urns, painted Attic vases. Opposite the Cathedral is the Bishop's Palace, linked to the church by means of a portico. The church of **San Francesco** (13th century), with its Romanesque façade and double flight of steps is also most interesting; the columns of the portal are 10th century, whilst the architrave is Roman. In the immediate environs of the town, scattered around the countryside, one can visit a number of important Etruscan tombs (one can ask for a guided tour at the museum). The **tomb of the Pellegrina** (3rd-2nd century B.C.) still possesses its funerary furnishings, with fine examples of cinerary urns and a sarcophagus. The **tomb of the Monkey** (Scimmia - 5th century) is renowned for its wall paintings: banqueting scenes, wrestlers chariot races and other games that were played during the funeral ceremonies in the Etruscan world. The **tomb of the Grand Duke** (3rd-2nd century) contains a number of cinerary urns decorated in relief with mythological figures.

Chiusi - The Cathedral; below: the entrance to the National Etruscan Museum.

AREZZO

Arezzo was a major Etruscan and, in the following period, Roman center. The great rival of Florence and Siena, it reached the height of power in the early 1300s under the *Signoria* of Guido Tarlati, (by the end of the century, however, it had become a dominion of Florence). The homeland of a number of famous men (Petrarch, Piero della Francesca, Michelangelo, and Vasari among them), Arezzo today is an active city with a picturesque medieval downtown section. Its economic mainstays are agriculture, ready-to-wear, and jewelry. It hosts the popular *Giostra del Saracino*, a tournament in medieval costume, the first Sunday of September.

Arezzo - The apse of the Parish Church of Santa Maria.

RECOMMENDED ITINERARIES – Start your tour of historic Arezzo in **Piazza Grande** (the apse section of the **Pieve di Santa Maria** faces out on the square), and then turn left into *Corso Italia*. Take Via Cavour on the right to **San Francesco** and then Via Cesalpino opposite the church which ascends to the **Cathedral**. The street front of the Duomo, *Passeggio del Prato*, leads to the 16th century *Fort*, while going left on Via Ricasoli, then Via Sassoverde you reach **San Domenico**. Then take Via San Domenico on the left, go left down *Via XX Settembre* (along which is the house in which Vasari was born) and proceed until you reach the **Galleria e Museo Medievale e Moderno** on the right side of *Canto alla Croce*. On Via Margaritone, outside the historic section, are the *Roman amphitheater* and the **Mecenate Archeological Museum**.

PIAZZA GRANDE – The irregular shaped square is bordered by buildings dating from different periods. The most important are the porticoed *Palazzo delle Logge* by Vasari, *Palazzo della Fraternita dei Laici*, which is half Gothic (lower section) and half Renaissance (upper section), the 17th century *Court Building*, and the Romanesque apse of the Pieve.

Chiusi - NATIONAL ETRUSCAN MUSEUM; from left to right and from top to bottom: capital, one of the rooms, female bust; sarcophagus from the Tomb of the Pellegrina.

Arezzo - The Piazza Grande with the apse of the Parish Church of Santa Maria overlooking it.

PIEVE DI SANTA MARIA – Built between 1140 and the early 1300s, the church ranks as one of the outstanding examples of Tuscan Romanesque architecture extant.

Its rectangular facade is adorned with Pisan style arcading and superb 13th century sculpture (*central portal*). Alongside is an unusual belltower pierced by forty Gothic windows. The single-aisle interior has the raised choir-lowered crypt plan typical of Tuscan Romanesque. Some great works are displayed inside: a superb *altarpiece* by Pietro Lorenzetti over the main altar, a *Crucifix* by Margaritone d'Arezzo (sacristy door), a 14th century silver *reliquary* (Cappella del Sacramento), and a 14th century *baptismal font* (right aisle).

SAN FRANCESCO – This simple brick and stone church, typical of the Franciscan Gothic style, was built between the late 13th and 14th centuries.

Inside is a celebrated fresco cycle, the *Legend of the True Cross*, painted by Piero della Francesca between 1453 and 1464. Among the most famous scenes are *King Solomon's Meeting with the Queen of Sheba*, the *Dream of Constantine*, and the *Finding of the True Cross*. The right wall of the church, with its Gothic and Renaissance altars, still has part of its 14th-15th century fresco decoration. Other noteworthy features are a *Crucifixion* by Spinello Aretino, an *Annunciation* attributed to Signorelli, and a 13th century crucifix. The lower church, reached by a staircase, dates from the 13th-14th centuries.

CATHEDRAL – Although work on the building was begun around the late 1200s, the project was finished only in the early 16th century, while the facade is actually a modern work (1914). The lovely Gothic *portal* on the right side dates from the 14th century. The interior, illuminated by superb 16th century *stained glass windows* designed by Guillaume de Marcillat, vaults a fresco by Piero della Francesca of *Mary Magdalene* (left aisle), as well as 16th century frescoes (*Cappella Tarlati*), and a medieval tomb, that of Bishop Tarlati dated 1330.

SAN DOMENICO – This late 13th century Romanesque-Gothic church has some fine paintings: 14th and 15th century frescoes (those by Spinello Aretino are of especial note) and a great *Crucifix* by Cimabue over the main altar dated 1265.

GALLERIA E MUSEO MEDIEVALE E MODERNO – The museum building is a 15th century palace, *Palazzo Bruni-Ciocchi*, attributed to Rossellino. Among the important works on display are a *St. Francis* by Margaritone d'Arezzo, an *Angel* by Guariento, works by followers of Spinello Aretino, a terracotta of the *Madonna di Misericordia* by Bernardo Rossellino, two paintings of *St. Roch* by Bartolomeo della Gatta, a *Virgin and Saints* attributed to Luca Signorelli, a *Virgin* by Rosso Fiorentino, as well as works by Vasari and some 19th century Macchiaioli school painters. Another outstanding feature of the museum is the *maiolica collection* (13th, 14th and 15th century Spanish, and Italian Renaissance pieces).

MECENATE ARCHEOLOGICAL MUSEUM – The museum is housed in an old monastery (15th-16th century *Monastero di San Bernardo*), situated near Arezzo's *Roman amphitheater* (1st-2nd century B.C.). The collection is divided into two sections, Etruscan and Roman. The Etruscan collection comprises urns, figurines and other terracotta sculptures, and vases. There are also Greek works, e.g. a superb 5th-4th century B.C. vase with a scene of the *Battle of the Amazons*. The Roman collection features the so-called ''*coral vases*,'' typical of the Arezzo region, as well as mosaics, weapons, and sculpture. Other exhibits pertain to the Italic tribes.

The Parish Church of Santa Maria with its majestic bell tower, below: San Francesco.

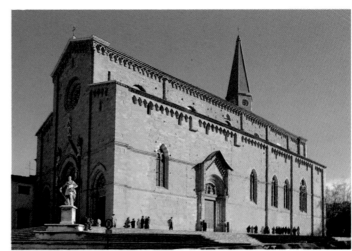

The Cathedral; below: San Domenico.

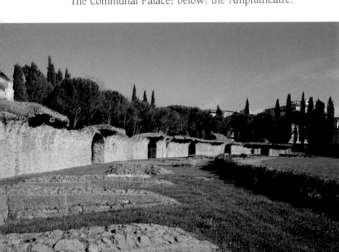

The Communal Palace; below: the Amphitheatre.

Santa Maria delle Grazie.

THE PROVINCE OF AREZZO

1. The Casentino and the Monasteries — 2. The Tiber Valley — 3. The Valdarno and Pratomagno.

1. THE CASENTINO AND THE MONASTERIES

This itinerary winds through the Casentino, a lush green valley - where the upper course of the Arno river flows through fertile pastures, vineyards and, in the hilly and mountainous areas, beneath fir-tree plantations. Leaving Arezzo, one proceeds northwards along state road Nr. 71, towards Bibbiena; at Rassina, one turns right and climbs up to the Verna.

THE VERNA – The monastery, one of the most renowned and visited Franciscan sanctuaries, derives its name from the mountain upon which it is situated, between the two groups of the Appennine range, called the Alpe di Serra and the Alpe di Catenaia.

In 1213, St. Francis was given the mountain by Count Orlando Cattani and founded a small community, together with a handful of followers there, the following year, building a few wattle huts for them all to live in. He returned many times to visit the community of recluses and it was here, in the month of September in 1224, that the "poor friar of Assisi" received his stigmata; after this event the Verna became an important monastery, and began to be visited by innumerable devoted pilgrims. A clearing looking out over a magnificent view surrounds the little church of **Santa Maria degli Angeli** (of the Angels), which has been restructured innumerable times since it was first founded in 1216; from the aisleless interior, containing fine Della Robbia terracotta reliefs, one enters the 15th century rooms of the **Museum of the Sanctuary** containing detached frescoes and various instances of the Minor Arts, mostly from the 15th and 16th centuries. The Greater Church (**Chiesa Maggiore**), built at a later date (14th-15th century), has an aisleless interior, containing remarkable Della Robbia terracotta reliefs (see the admirable *Adoration of the Child* and the *Annunciation*). The porch in front of the church (built at the beginning of the 16th century, but almost completely reconstructed after the last war) is where the procession of monks passes every afternoon at 3 p.m. as it proceeds chanting towards the *chapel of the Stigmata*, to pray there: in the floor, a stone protected by a sheet of glass recalls the spot where the miracle took place. One can also visit the monastery, that has grown over the centuries and now comprises five interesting cloisterways (the central, 16th century one is particularly fine, as well as the two leading into the inner guest house).

From the Verna one can get to Camaldoli, by a tortuous road that clambers up the Alpe di Serra, to Badia Prataglia and continues through the Fangacci pass. It is easier, however, to return to state road Nr. 71 and proceed along it until Serravalle, where one bears left.

HERMITAGE OF CAMALDOLI – The ancient monastic complex is at the heart of a miraculously undamaged forest of ancient fir trees; the Mother House of the Camaldolese Order has its hermitage near the top of the mountain, at an altitude of 1104 ms., whereas the actual monastery building is lower down (816 ms.).

The hermitage, to which the monastery was added later, was founded in 1012 by St. Romualdus, upon land donated to him by Count Maldolo in Arezzo, whence the name Camaldoli. Hermits still live up in the twenty cells immersed in the mystical silence of the thick forest — the most ancient cells date back to the 12th century, the most recent to the 17th — devoting their lives to prayer and meditation. In a small courtyard outside the secluded area, is a church, founded in the 11th century, but restructured many times during the following centuries, with an 18th century façade, flanked by two bell towers, with a Baroque interior decorated with golden stucco-work. The monastery, which was conceived originally as a hospice and guest house, was rebuilt in the 13th century; later on, after various vicissitudes, it continued to grow, becoming, moreover, a great cultural centre (even today, it is used for conventions and cultural events). There are three main sections: the monastery proper, the church and the guest house. The monastery, with a fine 17th century refectory, occupies the upper storey; in the ancient guest house, or Hospitium Camalduli, where the guests of the monastery are allowed to stay, is an 11th century

Sanctuary of the Verna - The interior; below: the Chapel of the Stigmata.

Bibbiena - The church of the Saints Hippolitus and Donatus.

The exterior of the Sanctuary of the Verna; below, right: **Poppi** - The Praetorian Palace or Castle of the Counts Guidi.

Poppi - Monument to Dante Alighieri. Below: **Bibbiena** - The Sanctuary of Santa Maria del Sasso.

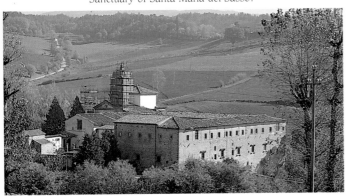

courtyard with a fine portico as well as a small 15th century cloister. The church that was restructured in the 16th century and enlarged in the 17th, possesses a Baroque aisleless interior, containing a number of paintings by Vasari; the cloister of the church is 16th century. The library is of Medieval aspect and very interesting; see also the typically 16th century dispensary.

The two most important centres in the valley are Bibbiena and Poppi. **Bibbiena** is the most dynamic agricultural and industrial centre in the Casentino area. The Arno runs through the town, which is divided into two sections: the more ancient part, at the top of the hill and a more recently built part at its foot. Almost certainly founded by the Etruscans, it was taken over by the Florentines in the Middle Ages. It was the birthplace of Bernardo Dovizi, known as Bibbiena, who was secretary to Leo X and a well known man of letters. The more ancient part is full of fine monuments like **Palazzo Dovizi** (15th century), the church, situated opposite, of **San Lorenzo** (15th century), the church of Saints Hippolytus and Donatus (**Ippolito e Donato**), founded at the beginning of 12th century and many times restructured subsequently (a recent restoration mostly carried out on the interior has brought some of the 14th-15th century structure to light). Just outside the town one finds the sanctuary of **Santa Maria del Sasso** (on the Stone), which was restructured in the Renaissance style at the end of the 15th century. A little to the north of Bibbiena, along state road Nr. 70, is **Poppi**, a picturesque little town, in the centre of the Casentino area, with its massive ancient castle towering above it. Once domain of the Counts Guidi, whose most representative residence it was, it became a part of the Florentine territories in the 15th century. The **Praetorian Castle** (or Castle of the Counts Guidi), with its high tower and powerful battlemented walls, was built between the 13th and 14th centuries; in perfect condition: the inner courtyard's walls are covered with the badges of the Florentine commissioners and delegates who resided in it; to the right, an open staircase mounts up to the upper storeys, and to a series of wooden gangways. See also some of the rooms and the chapel, with 14th century frescoes of the Florentine School.

Proceeding towards Florence, one encounters Borgo alla Collina, where one turns left and after passing through **Montemignaio**, an ancient hamlet and holiday resort, surrounded by thick chestnut woods, one gets to Vallombrosa.

VALLOMBROSA
– A summer and winter holiday and sports resort, in the heart of a thick forest of ancient trees on the slopes of Pratomagno, it has grown up around the ancient Benedictine monastery (the Vallombrosan Order follows the Rule of St. Benedict, although they have their own special regulations), which took its name from the place on which it stands.

The abbey was founded in 1051 by St. John Gualberto, a noble Florentine who decided to embrace a life of poverty and repentance. It has grown over the centuries and has been restructured many times. Its present aspect is due to the transformations effected in the 17th century, but the 13th century bell tower and the 15th century tower are still extant. The monastery is surrounded by a thick fir-tree forest that belongs to the State (known as the State's Fir Plantation = Abetina Demaniale) which also comprises an experimental tree nursery. An excursion to the **Paradisino**, which is a reconstruction of an 11th century hermitage, is worthwhile.

2. THE TIBER VALLEY (VALTIBERINA)

Leaving Arezzo, one proceeds eastwards, towards Umbria and, after the pass of the Scopetone, one follows the course of the Cerfone river and enters the valley of the Tiber, where one encounters Monterchi.

MONTERCHI
– Founded in the 11th century, it is a delightful little village perched at the top of a hill, which is still protected by its ancient walls as well as boasting a curious Medieval tunnel behind the parish church, the original Romanesque structure of which is no longer visible, due to the damage dealt to it over the centuries and to the massive reconstruction work carried out in the 1960s.

The most remarkable artistic treasure of the area, however, is the superb detached fresco by Piero della Francesca in the little chapel next to the cemetery, just outside the village; painted around 1445, the *Madonna del Parto* (Childbirth) is one of the most luminous examples of Renaissance painting. Just before Monterchi, the turning, off to the left, leads to Anghiari.

Sansepolcro - The Cathedral; below: the Palace of the Lauds, used today as Town Hall.

Monterchi - View of the little Medieval burg. Below: **Anghiari** - View.

ANGHIARI – An agricultural and industrial centre, with an old section surrounded by fortifications at the top of the hill and a more recently built part spread over the lower lying ground.

The old part of the town is full of charming corners and picturesque alleys, winding around its stone Medieval dwellings and handsome Renaissance palaces. The 18th century church of **Santa Maria delle Grazie** contains a fine panel by Antonio Sogliani, depicting the *Last Supper* (1531); the asymmetrical interior of the Medieval church of **Badia**, greatly restructured over the centuries, since its foundation in the early 11th century, is definitely intriguing. Handsome **Palazzo Taglieschi**, built during the Renaissance, contains the **State Museum of Popular Arts and Traditions of the Upper Tiber Valley**, where one can admire a variety of artistic objects from the churches and buildings of the Anghiari and Tiber Valley areas, as well as an interesting collection of objects and utensils illustrating the ancient habits and customs of the local population. Just outside the town, one finds the ancient **parish church of Sovara**, founded in the 9th/10th century (careful restoration has recaptured its early Romanesque structure), as well as the beautiful church of **Santa Maria a Corsano** (13th century) with its distinctive bell tower based on French architectural models.

Not far away, on the other side of the Tiber, is Sansepolcro.

SANSEPOLCRO – A commercial centre, in which a large number of firms have sited their industrial plants, situated in the Upper Tiber Valley beneath the Alpe della Luna (Mountain of the Moon).

The historical centre, of 15th-16th century aspect, revolves around Piazza di Torre di Berta (which used to have a Medieval tower in the middle of it, that was destroyed during the last war) and Via Matteotti, with its 14th/15th century tower-mansions, along which one finds the **Cathedral**, a Romanesque-Gothic structure, founded in the 11th century and restructured and restored several times in the course of time (the façade, which has benefited the most from the restoration, possesses a fine recessed portal, surmounted by a great rose-window). The restored and restructured building that contains the **Civic Museum** is a 14th century construction (to which access can be gained from Via Aggiunti) and abuts on Via Matteotti too. It contains, among other things: important works by Piero della Francesca who was born in Sansepolcro (the frescoed *Resurrection*, the *Madonna of Mercy*, a frescoed *St. Ludovic* and the *bust of a saint*), as well as fine paintings by Luca Signorelli and Pontormo (a remarkable *St. Quentin*). Again on Via Matteotti, we find the **Palace of the Lauds**, now the seat of the Town Hall, which was built between the 16th and 17th century, with a fine inner courtyard, and the **Praetorian Palace**, founded in the 14th century and restructured in the 19th century, with a façade decorated with the badges of the Captains and Bailiffs who used to reside in the palace. The nearby church of **San Francesco** (late 13th century) is also interesting; opposite: the charming church of the **Madonna delle Grazie** (of Favours) founded in the 16th century.

Proceeding along the Upper Tiber valley road, one reaches Ranchi, whereupon, taking the turning on the right, one reaches Cortona.

CORTONA – An agricultural centre and an important meeting point for antique dealers (a famous Antique Dealers Fair is held here every year in August and September), possessing rich artistic and environmental resources. Luca Signorelli and Pietro da Cortona were both born here.

The walls (part of which still reveal Etruscan sections) protect the entrancing Medieval nucleus, with steep, twisting lanes and houses with the upper storeys overhanging the streets, supported on wooden corbels. The central Piazza della Repubblica is surrounded by a number of Medieval buildings, including the 13th century **Communal Palace**, that was enlarged in the 16th century (the battlemented tower was built in 1509) and underwent a somewhat infelicitous restoration at the end of the last century. In nearby Piazza Signorelli, we find the **Praetorian Palace**, whose original 13th century structure is still visible along the flank, covered with badges, and, in part, in the inner courtyard, whereas the façade reveals the alterations carried out in the 17th century. The palace contains the **Museum of the Etruscan Academy**, that assembles a large number of very interesting Etruscan finds, such as the great richly decorated *bronze lamp* of the 5th century B.C. as well as other testimonials of past civilisations, like the Roman and Egyptian cultures (see the 12th dynasty funeral river boat), not to mention a number of valuable Medieval and

Cortona - The Communal Palace.

Cortona - The Cathedral; below: San Francesco.

Cortona - View; below, left: pillar with capital, once part of the earlier Cathedral, still visible on the façade of the later building.

Cortona - The Signorelli Theatre, with, to the left, the Praetorian Palace; below: the church of the Madonna del Calcinaio.

Renaissance works. The **Cathedral**, that was rebuilt in the 16th century is in the centre of the square named after it (Piazza del Duomo) and is reputed to have been built by Giuliano da Sangallo (see the fine doorway on the right flank). The **Diocesan Museum** also looks out onto the square and contains remarkable paintings by Fra Angelico (a magnificent *Annunciation*) and Luca Signorelli, as well as other fine works by Tuscan masters. There are a number of interesting churches, such as: the sanctuary of **Santa Margherita** (rebuilt in the 19th century), containing the fine 14th century tomb of St. Margaret; the church of **San Francesco**, founded in the 13th century and restructured in the 17th century, where one can admire a fascinating Byzantine reliquary of the 10th century; the church of **San Nicolò**, containing a remarkable standard, painted by Signorelli. Three kms. from the town, one comes to the church of the **Madonna del Calcinaio** (of the Lime-pit - 15th-16th century), a marvellous example of Renaissance architecture by Francesco di Giorgio Martini.

Cortona - The sanctuary of Santa Margherita.

3. THE VALDARNO AND THE PRATOMAGNO

One takes the state road 69 in the direction of Florence, and proceeds along the wide, populous valley of the Arno, surrounded by typically Tuscan olive groves and vineyards, separated every now and then, by woods; attractive farm-steads stud the landscape, at the top of every hill and rise.

MONTEVARCHI – An agricultural and industrial township, one of the most active market towns in Tuscany and already renowned as a trading post in the Middle Ages. It is the gathering point for all the Palaeological finds dug up all over the Arno Valley.

During the Medici Grand Ducal period, it had already developed a flourishing textile industry. The **Collegiata di San Lorenzo** (the main church) is a building founded in the 13th century and totally rebuilt in the 18th century, with a monumental Baroque altar surmounted by a *Madonna in Glory*, by Giovanni Baratta. The adjoining **Museum**, in the old sacristy, with a majestic Della Robbia *shrine*, removed from the church in the 18th century, when the reconstruction took place, as well as various examples of the Minor Arts of the 14th and 15th centuries. The **Palaeontological Museum** in the ex-monastery of San Ludovico, is particularly interesting, inasmuch as it possesses animal and vegetable fossils mostly unearthed in the Upper Arno Valley.

Proceeding northwards, one comes to a turning on the left that leads up to the **convent of Montecarlo**, a solitary Renaissance monastery containing a fine *Annunciation*, by Fra Angelico. Continuing onwards one comes to **Cavriglia**, where there is an unusual wild-life park-zoo. State road 69, on the other hand, leads to San Giovanni.

SAN GIOVANNI VALDARNO – The town, founded by Florence in 1296, has developed, spreading out to cover the plain on the left bank of the Arno; it is the largest industrial centre in the area (the lignite deposits in the surrounding hills are most important). One of the greatest painters of the Renaissance, Masaccio, was born here.

The ancient centre of the town which was designed, according to tradition, by the famous architect and sculptor, Arnolfo di Cambio, is a rationally planned rectangle crossed longitudinally by long straight roads and contains a number of interesting buildings. The **Praetorian Palace**, attributed to Arnolfo di Cambio, but considerably restructured, is surrounded on all sides by an uninterrupted portico; its walls are covered with the badges of the podestàs and delegates who inhabited the palace in the 15th and 16th centuries; the basilica of **Santa Maria delle Grazie**, built in the 15th century, has a 19th century façade, with a portico that protects a glazed terracotta relief by Giovanni della Robbia; the 17th century interior, with a nave flanked by two side-aisles, contains among other things, a number of Renaissance works of art.

From San Giovanni, as from Montevarchi, a series of roads wind up to the hills along the left bank of the Arno, towards **Pratomagno**, which extends its hilly contours between Florence and Arezzo, separating the Valdarno from the Casentino. The highest peak is the Croce di Pratomagno (1592 ms.). One of the main centers of the area is **Terranuova Bracciolini**, with its ancient fortifications; see also: **Loro Ciuffenna** with the nearby **parish church of Gropina**: an early Christian edifice built on top of a pre-Christian temple, partially restructured in the Romanesque period and renowned for its capitals decorated with odd symbolic figures; **Castelfranco di Sopra** that preserves the lay-out given to it at the end of the 13th century by Arnolfo di Cambio.

Montevarchi - The Collegiata of San Lorenzo; below: the cloisters.

INDEX